VICKI COBB

SCIENCE EXPERIMENTS YOU CAN EAT

REVISED & UPDATED

ILLUSTRATED BY
TAD CARPENTER

HARPER
An Imprint of HarperCollinsPublishers

IMPORTANT SAFETY NOTE: This book contains experiments that may be dangerous, and all of the experiments in this book should be carried out under adult supervision only. In particular, many of the experiments involve use of a stove, oven, lighters, matches, or chemicals, may be unsafe for those with food allergies, or may otherwise be inherently dangerous. This book also contains nutritional information, which, while carefully researched and all efforts made to ensure its accuracy as of the date published, should by no means be considered a substitute for the advice of a qualified health professional. The author and publisher expressly disclaim responsibility for any injury, damages, or adverse effects that result from following the information or engaging in the experiments contained in this book.

Science Experiments You Can Eat (revised edition)

Text copyright © 1972, 1994, 2016 by Vicki Cobb

Illustrations copyright © 2016 by Tad Carpenter

All rights reserved. Manufactured in the United States of America.

No part of this book may be used or reproduced in any manner whatsoever without written permission except in the case of brief quotations embodied in critical articles and reviews. For information address HarperCollins Children's Books, a division of HarperCollins Publishers, 195 Broadway, New York, NY 10007. www.harpercollinschildrens.com

Library of Congress Cataloging-in-Publication Data

Names: Cobb, Vicki, author. | Carpenter, Tad, illustrator.

Title: Science experiments you can eat / Vicki Cobb ; illustrations, Tad Carpenter.

Description: Revised and updated [edition]. | New York, NY : Harper, an imprint of HarperCollins Publishers, [2016] | "First Edition." | Audience: Ages 8-12.

Identifiers: LCCN 2015046347 | ISBN 9780062377296 (pbk.)

Subjects: LCSH: Food—Experiments—Juvenile literature. | Science—Experiments—Juvenile literature. | Cooking—Juvenile literature. | Science projects—Juvenile literature.

Classification: LCC Q164 .C52 2016 | DDC 507.8—dc23

Typography and design by Carpenter Collective

17 18 19 20 21   LSC/C   10 9 8 7 6 5 4

Originally published in 1972 by Harper Trophy

First revised and updated edition, 1994

Second revised and updated edition, 2016

TO THE MEMORY OF MY PARENTS:

Paula Wolf, for whom cooking was an act of love

Benjamin Wolf, the inspirational autodidact, who
mastered so many things by reading books

AND FOR MY GRANDCHILDREN:

Abby, Lexi, Ben, Jonny, and Jillian, who inherit the
legacy of three generations of lifelong learners

CONTENTS

HUNGRY?

Chew on this. Once you've taken care of your need for food, what else are you hungry for? Personally, I'm always hungry to learn, to share what I've learned, and to create. That's why I'm a scientist and a writer. Maybe you are, too. The most exciting things to come out of science and creativity are those amazing "aha" moments—the triumphant feeling that comes when you just know you've "gotten it." This book is the result of one such moment. A friend phoned me to suggest that we collaborate on a cookbook for kids. We both had young families at the time and cooked every day. I remember thinking to myself, "I don't want to write a cookbook. I want to write about science for kids." And then, the title *Science Experiments You Can Eat* popped into my head. There is nothing more amazing than having an idea pop into your head—especially when you know you can act on it. This "aha" moment gave me a vision for this book. I would use activities with food to help kids discover basic principles of science. I would create a tool so that you, too, could make discoveries and have many "aha" moments of your own.

Scientific discoveries have long influenced what shows up on your plate at mealtimes. Agronomy, the science of how food is grown, has helped farmers produce bigger and better crops. Methods of food preservation allow food storage for out-of-season consumption. Food additives and food packaging technologies, developed by scientists and engineers, maintain crispness, moistness, texture, flavor, visual appeal, and shelf life for thousands of different food products. There is virtually no chance of a famine in developed countries. That's the good news.

The bad news is that the science of nutrition, which determines standards for a healthy diet, publishes new studies from time to time that tell us that a food we thought was good for us, or at least safe for consumption, can create health problems in the long run. Currently, 70 percent of the American diet is made up of processed food—food that has been manufactured to give it a longer shelf life and to make it taste "crave-able" so you can't eat just one bite. Modern life is so hectic that many families don't sit down together every evening to share dinner and conversation. One result of these changes is an obesity epidemic among children. So, in this new edition of *Science Experiments You Can Eat*, I have added a chapter about some of the influences of science on foods we do eat. It will help you read between the lines of the Nutrition Facts labels so that you understand the importance of healthy choices in your own diet. In addition, I have included nutrition information throughout the other chapters of the book as you also learn basic physics, chemistry, and biology.

But mostly this book is designed to whet your appetite for science. I want it to nourish your curiosity and feed your mind. I want to make science not only digestible but a feast of discovery. This book is a banquet of ideas and processes and yes, some very tasty and some not-so-tasty results. (Although I've done every experiment, to be honest, I haven't eaten them all.) This is not gourmet dining, but it is food for thought.

PLAYING WITH FOOD

Cookbooks give you precise directions for preparing food. Recipes are the result of many experiments in test kitchens that turn out predictable, delicious dishes.

But this is a science book, *not* a cookbook. Food preparation produces a lot of changes in food. And *change* is what interests scientists.

There is no simpler activity for a cook than boiling water. Put water in a pot, put it over a burner on the stove, and wait for bubbles to form. But a scientist looks at this phenomenon and asks many questions: How hot does water have to be in order to boil? Does the temperature of water still rise after it starts boiling? If not, why not? Does water boil at a different temperature at sea level compared to in the mountains? If so, what does that tell us about this phenomenon? What is steam? How can steam be used to power, say, a locomotive? Scientific understanding of boiling water was one of the great breakthroughs in science and technology. The purpose of this book is to get you to think as a scientist. It will also help you as a cook. You will come to understand that science is not the mysterious process for eggheads it's cracked up to be.

So when you do these experiments, keep an open mind. You'll get ideas. You'll start wondering. And, best of all, you may start asking questions that you can answer with experiments of your own. If that happens, you might just be on your way to one of those precious "aha" moments. So don't dismiss the power of your own brain. Good questions are how science makes progress. Here's what Einstein, the most amazing scientist of the twentieth century and the icon of "genius," said about questions: "If I had an hour to solve a problem and my life depended on the solution, I would spend the first fifty-five minutes determining the proper question to ask, for once I know the proper question, I could solve the problem in less than five minutes." And "To raise new questions, new possibilities, to regard old problems from a new angle requires creative imagination and marks real advances in science."

The best way to get ideas is to do something. This book is a good place to begin. If you don't get the results you expect, it is *not* a failure. Nature doesn't lie. Your results depend on many variables—the equipment and ingredients you used and the procedures you followed. I've tried to give you directions in this book that will yield predictable results. But your kitchen is not my kitchen. If you don't get the expected results, try to think of what factors might have caused the difference. Redesign and repeat the procedure and see what happens. This is something scientists do—they publish their procedures so that others may repeat their experiments to make sure they all get the same data. In this way, science corrects itself. The body of knowledge that we call "science" is the result of countless experiments by many people. Imagine that! A community of people produced this knowledge and shared it with the world. Free! Science is the original wiki. Now you can join that community with experiments of your own.

Did you know scientists love to play? They've never forgotten what it's like to be a kid. "Play" means that you suspend the rules and try stuff just for fun, just to see what happens. This book is your excuse to do just that.

HOW TO USE THIS BOOK

In order to ask good questions, you need some background knowledge. So every chapter in this book has a short introduction that discusses the subject you will be investigating. Every experiment also has a short introduction that asks a question you can answer by doing the experiment. If you skip these, you might as well go use a cookbook. Before you begin any experiment, you need to know *what* you are doing and *why* you are doing it.

If you don't have a lot of background in science, if you've never heard of molecules, solutions, elements, compounds, and chemical reactions, you can use this book as Science 101 and go through each chapter in order. If you like to plunge right in, begin by browsing and find an experiment that captures your imagination. I intend this book to be fun . . . not a chore. No rules here!

The materials and equipment needed are listed at the beginning of each experiment. Collect everything before you begin. This way you will not be caught without some important item at a critical time during the experiment. For the most part, I use materials that are easy to find at your local supermarket. But there are a few experiments that require ingredients or equipment that you can find easily online at low cost. This means you might have to wait a few days before you can start. So planning and waiting may be part of the process.

The procedure section tells you how to do the experiment. Often, the reasons for doing a certain step are discussed as you go along. Since timing is important, you should read and understand the whole procedure section before you start the experiment.

There are certain standard practices for safety and use of equipment in every laboratory, and your kitchen is no exception. Consult the cook in your house before you start experimenting, and ask for help with any procedures you are not sure about.

After the procedure section, there is a brief discussion of what your results mean. Often I have included questions to help direct you in your observations. I don't always tell you what your results should be. This gives you the opportunity to get answers for yourself from your experiments, just as real scientists do.

As you do these experiments, questions of your own will occur to you. Take notes! Honor your questions! Don't worry that you are getting sidetracked. Believe it or not, finding something interesting and getting sidetracked is the goal of every working scientist. Your own discoveries are what make science an adventure! This book is your road map. Bon voyage and bon appétit!

SOLUTIONS

The "stuff" that makes up food, you, and everything else in the universe is called *matter*. Chemists are scientists who study matter and how it changes. Matter is anything that has weight and takes up space.

When scientists first tackled the study of matter, they had to deal with the problem that matter in its natural state is complicated. Most matter exists mixed up with other matter. (Perhaps the most famous example of pure stuff is gold. It is called a "noble metal" because it doesn't react with most other substances and is found pure in nature.) A *solution*, such as seawater, is an especially interesting kind of mixture. One amazing thing about a solution is that it is evenly mixed or *homogeneous*. In a pail of seawater, a cup taken from the top has exactly the same amount of salt in it as a cup taken from the bottom. Another amazing feature of solutions is that they become homogeneous *all by themselves*. No stirring is necessary.

Chemists have a way of thinking—a model—about solutions that accounts for their interesting properties. They say that solutions, like all matter, are made up of tiny particles too small to see. These particles are arranged in two phases. One phase is called the *solvent*. Water is the most common solvent around. The solvent phase is *continuous*. This means that the water particles are in contact with one another. The other phase is called the *solute*. Salt is a solute in seawater. The solute phase is *discontinuous*. Solute particles may occasionally bump into one another but for the most part they are surrounded by solvent particles. Salt water that you mix yourself in your kitchen is a simple solution, which means it has one solvent and one solute. But seawater has a number of solutes, including sodium bicarbonate (baking soda) and calcium carbonate (lime). A solution may be made of one or more solvents and one or more solutes.

When a solute dissolves, the solute particles move through the solvent in a process called *diffusion*. You don't even have to stir. See for yourself. Drop a lump of sugar (a solute) into a glass of water (a solvent) and let it stand for a while. What happens to the lump of sugar? When you can no longer see any sugar crystals, taste the top of the solution with a straw. If sugar is present, you'll taste it. Use the straw to taste the solution near the bottom of the glass. To do this, cover the top end of the straw with your finger before you lower the other end into the solution. When the bottom of the straw is where you want to take your sample, carefully flex your finger to let a small amount of the solution rise into the straw. Keep your finger on the top of the straw as you raise the bottom end of the straw to your mouth. Lift your finger to let the solution run into your mouth. With this technique you can taste samples from all parts of the solution. But be careful to keep the disturbance to the solution as little as possible when you insert the straw. Is the solution homogeneous? If it isn't, wait awhile and taste again.

Solutions are important in the study of matter. You can often discover what a substance is by the solvent it dissolves in and by how much of it dissolves. Many chemical reactions take place in solutions that will not take place in air. Life is only possible because of solutions. The human body is 50 to 75 percent water, and most of the chemical reactions in your body take place in solution. This chapter will introduce you to some different solutions and some of the ways solutions are used to learn about matter.

ROCK CANDY

RECOVERING SOLUTE CRYSTALS

It's easy to separate a solute from its solvent if you don't care about keeping the solvent. Leave a water solution open to the air and the solvent will evaporate, leaving the solute behind. To recover the solute from all kinds of beverages, put small amounts in shallow dishes. The water evaporates from the large surface area.

Some solutes form *crystals* as the solvent evaporates. Crystals are solids that have a regular geometric shape, with many sides or faces. Take a close look at sugar and salt crystals with a magnifying lens. They have very different shapes.

Rock candy is simply very large sugar crystals. Grow some in the next experiment.

MATERIALS & EQUIPMENT

- ½ cup water

- 1 cup sugar

- a measuring cup

- a small saucepan

- a wooden spoon

- a magnifying glass

- 3 or 4 small shallow dishes (aluminum foil muffin cups work well)

PROCEDURE

1 Pour the water into the saucepan. Measure out a cup of sugar. Put just a spoonful of this sugar in the water and stir. Use a wooden spoon to stir; it won't get hot the way a metal spoon would when you heat this solution later. Continue to add sugar by the spoonful, stirring after each addition until the sugar dissolves. How many spoonfuls before the sugar stops dissolving no matter how much you stir? When this happens the solution is called a *saturated solution*.

2 Set the saucepan on the stove over low heat for a few minutes. What happens to the undissolved crystals as the solution gets warmer?

3 Turn off the heat and remove the saucepan from the stove. Add sugar again, spoonful by spoonful. How many spoonfuls do you need to make a saturated solution in hot water?

4 Pour all the remaining sugar from the measuring cup into the saucepan. Put the saucepan on the stove again and continue heating gently until all the sugar has dissolved. Then bring it to the boiling point and boil for about a minute. The solution should be thick and clear and contain no sugar crystals. Pour the solution carefully into the small dishes while it is hot. It's not important to distribute the solution evenly.

OBSERVATIONS

Watch the solution as it cools. Be careful not to jolt it or disturb it in any way. Does the solution remain clear? If it becomes cloudy, take a close look at it with a magnifying glass. A clear solution that contains more solute than would normally dissolve at that temperature is said to be *supersaturated*. Supersaturated solutions are very unstable and the slightest disturbance will cause crystals to form, removing them from the solution.

Some candy, like fudge, depends on the formation of millions of tiny crystals. When you beat fudge, tiny crystals form quickly from a supersaturated solution, as the extra solute comes out of the solution.

If you don't beat fudge hard enough, the crystals will be larger and the fudge will feel grainy in your mouth.

To make rock candy, you want large crystals to grow, and this takes time, sometimes weeks. Let the water-and-sugar solution stand undisturbed at room temperature for a week or more. Every day, carefully break off the crust of crystals that forms at the surface so that the water can continue to evaporate.

Rock candy crystals will form around any small object you put in the solution. Make rock candy lollipops by putting a swizzle stick in a glass of supersaturated sugar solution. Rock candy will also quickly form around a crystal of sugar dropped into the solution. Such a crystal is called a *seed crystal*. You might want to try using a colored crystal sprinkle as a seed crystal in a supersaturated solution.

The formation of crystals is one way chemists know when they've got pure matter, either an element or a compound. Crystals are also a clue to the structure of a substance. Scientists figure that the perfect shape of crystals is not an accident but is the result of a regular arrangement of the smallest particles of a substance. These particles, *atoms* and *molecules*, have a size (although they're way too small to see even with the strongest microscope) and a shape. The arrangement of the atoms or molecules of a crystal produces the shape of the crystal much as closely stacked bricks can produce only a rectangular stack.

Compare the shape of the rock candy crystals to the crystals of granulated sugar with a magnifying glass. Are they the same shape? Do sugar crystals have the same shape as salt crystals? Would you expect sugar molecules to have the same shape as salt molecules?

ICE POPS AND THE FREEZING POINT OF SOLUTIONS

One question that comes up over and over again in the laboratory is: How do you know when you have a pure substance? One way to answer this question is to see how a substance you know to be pure (usually because a manufacturer says so on the label) behaves differently from a substance you know to be a mixture (because you make it yourself). It's well established that pure water freezes at 32° Fahrenheit or 0° Celsius. Does a solution freeze at the same temperature as pure water? Do the next experiment and find out.

MATERIALS & EQUIPMENT

- 1 cup clear, not cloudy, canned or bottled fruit juice (cherry, grape, or apple work well)
- water
- 6 (5-ounce) paper cups

Continued . . .

- a pen
- 6 circles of cardboard big enough to cover the tops of the cups
- 6 swizzle sticks or wooden stirring sticks
- 2 measuring cups (each cup should hold at least 1 cup liquid)

PROCEDURE

To set up this experiment you will put different amounts of fruit juice in each cup in a systematic way and then freeze all the cups. The first ice pop will be undiluted fruit juice as it comes from the container, the second will be ½ fruit juice and ½ water, the third will be ¼ fruit juice and ¾ water, and so on. This systematic changing of the amount of water in a solution is called *serial dilution*. Laboratories in many industries use serial dilutions to test the strength of a substance to find out, for example, how much detergent to put into a washing machine or how much aspirin to take when you are sick.

Since this experiment compares the freezing point of the ice pops to the freezing point of pure water, you will also make an ice pop that is pure water, without juice. This ice pop is called the *control*. A control is treated just like every other part of an experiment but does not contain the thing being tested, so that it can be used as a basis for comparison.

1   Start by marking the cups: juice, ½, ¼, ⅛, $^1/_{16}$, and control.

2   The purpose of the cardboard circle covers is to hold each stick upright until the ice pop has frozen. The covers should be large enough to cover the tops of the cups without falling in. Punch a hole just large enough to insert a stick in the center of each cardboard circle. Place a stick in each hole.

3 Measure ½ cup of water and pour it into the cup marked "control."

4 Measure 1 cup of juice. Pour ½ cup of this juice into a second measuring cup. Then pour the remaining ½ cup of juice into the paper cup labeled "juice."

5 Add ½ cup of water to the second measuring cup to bring the volume up to 1 cup. Mix well. Use the first measuring cup to get ½ cup of this dilution. Pour this into the cup marked "½."

6 Add ½ cup of water to the first dilution to again bring the volume up to 1 cup. Mix well and use ½ cup of this dilution to make the next ice pop in the cup labeled "¼."

7 Follow the same procedure to make ice pops that are ⅛ juice and ¹⁄₁₆ juice.

8 Put a cover and stick on each cup. Adjust the sticks so they touch only the bottoms of the cups.

9 Put all six cups in your freezer. It is important to place them at the same depth so they will all be at the same temperature. After about 40 minutes, check to see how freezing is progressing by wiggling each stick back and forth. As freezing occurs, you can feel the ice forming. Keep checking about every 20 minutes.

Which pop freezes first? Which ice pop takes longest to freeze? Does it require more or less time to freeze a solution?

OBSERVATIONS

On the basis of your experiment, why is salt put on sidewalks in winter? Why is alcohol put in car radiators before the cold weather sets in? How can the temperature at which a solution freezes be used to tell how pure a substance is? Handbooks for chemists always list the freezing points of pure solvents. If they test the freezing point of a liquid in their lab and they don't get the freezing point they expect, they know that other substances must be present.

When the ice pops are frozen solid, which may take several hours, your experiment is completed and you may eat them. Although some of the ice pops will taste better than others, even the control can be refreshing on a hot day. Just tear off the paper cup and enjoy!

FRUIT DRINKS AND DISSOLVING RATES

Some solutions form more quickly than others. Can you think of some variables that cause this? In the next experiment, see how temperature affects the rate at which a solute dissolves in a solvent.

MATERIALS & EQUIPMENT

- ½ cup ice water
- ½ cup room-temperature water
- ½ cup boiling water
- 1 package of unsweetened Kool-Aid
- sugar
- 6½ cups cold water
- a measuring cup
- 3 clear glass tumblers
- a 2-quart pitcher

PROCEDURE

1 Put ½ cup of ice water in the first glass, ½ cup of room-temperature water in the second glass, and ½ cup of boiling water in the third glass.

2 Drop a small pinch of Kool-Aid into each glass. Watch how the Kool-Aid diffuses into solution.

OBSERVATIONS

In which glass does the Kool-Aid dissolve most quickly? How long does it take for the Kool-Aid to diffuse evenly through the water?

Try this with other colored solutes like instant coffee or food coloring.

After you have finished the experiment, you can prepare the Kool-Aid to drink. Pour all the solutions into a 2-quart pitcher. Add the remaining Kool-Aid and the amount of sugar suggested on the package. Add 6½ cups of cold water to bring the volume up to 2 quarts.

SOUR-BALL-ADE

How does the amount of surface area of a solute affect the rate at which it dissolves in a solvent? The next experiment explores this idea.

MATERIALS & EQUIPMENT

- ¾ cup room-temperature water

- 3 pieces of dark-colored hard candy (grape or cherry)

- 3 small glasses

- a measuring cup

- waxed paper

- a hammer or rolling pin

PROCEDURE

1 Pour ¼ cup of water into each glass.

2 Wrap one candy in waxed paper and tap it lightly with a hammer or rolling pin so it breaks into several large pieces. Wrap another candy in waxed paper and smash it so it is like granulated sugar.

3 Drop the whole candy into the first glass, the broken candy into the second glass, and the smashed candy into the third glass.

OBSERVATIONS

Which candy has the most surface area? Which candy dissolves first? How do you think the amount of surface area affects the rate at which a solute dissolves? How do your findings explain why superfine sugar is used to sweeten iced drinks?

You can make a refreshing drink from this experiment. Pour all three solutions into one glass and add a few ice cubes. An orange slice adds a festive touch.

RED CABBAGE INDICATOR

A sour taste is one indication of a type of solution called an *acid*. The word "acid" comes from a Latin word meaning sharp or biting to the taste. Acids also conduct electricity. A lightbulb connected by wires to two electrodes will light up when the electrodes are submerged in an acid. Acids are not the only solutions that conduct electricity. *Bases*, also called *alkalis*, do the job as well.

Acids are present in many of the foods we eat. Lemon juice and vinegar are good examples. We also eat certain bases, although they are not as common in food as acids. Baking soda, for example, is a base when it is dissolved in water.

There are, of course, many stronger acids and bases that we don't eat because they are poisonous or extremely damaging to living tissues. Tasting is not a test used by chemists to determine whether or not a substance is an acid or a base. Instead, they use a dye called an *indicator* that changes color depending on what the solution is. Litmus paper turns blue when it is dipped in a base and pink when it is dipped in an acid.

The pigment in red cabbage can be used as your own personal "litmus." Here's how to make some red cabbage indicator.

MATERIALS & EQUIPMENT

- 1 whole red cabbage
- water
- a knife
- 2 large bowls
- a grater (or food processor)
- measuring cups and spoons
- a slotted spoon
- a strainer
- a very clean glass jar and lid
- a small white dish

PROCEDURE

1   Cut the cabbage into quarters. Grate it section by section into a large bowl or chop it up in a food processor. Add between 1 and 2 cups of water to the bowl, enough to cover the cabbage. Let the cabbage stand in the water, stirring occasionally so that all the cabbage is moistened.

2   When the water is a strong red, remove as much of the grated cabbage as you can with the slotted spoon and save it in your second bowl. Pour the water solution through the strainer into the glass jar. Add the strained cabbage to the rest of the cabbage you have saved.

3   Put about a tablespoon of our cabbage-juice indicator into a small white dish. Test for an acid by adding a substance

you know to be an acid (like lemon juice or vinegar) to the cabbage juice. Notice the color it becomes in acid. Now use a fresh sample of cabbage juice and add a substance you know to be a base (baking soda). Again notice the color change. Pretty gorgeous! Now add acid to the base-and-indicator mixture to reverse the color change. What happens when you add base to the indicator showing the acid color? An acid and a base will react with each other to neutralize each other. The original color of the red cabbage is pretty close to neutral. Now you can test some foods to see which category they fall into, acids or bases. Here is a list to get you started:

- Cooking water from boiled vegetables, including beans, peas, onions, carrots, turnips, celery, asparagus, etc.

- Liquids from canned fruits and vegetables

- Cream of tartar

- Egg whites

- Fruit juices

- Cottage cheese

You can use the grated red cabbage raw in a salad or coleslaw, or you can experiment with it further. You must use it within two days or it will go bad.

MATERIALS & EQUIPMENT

- shredded cabbage from above experiment

- 1 tart apple

- water

- a knife

- a wooden spoon

- 2 aluminum pots (Check the underside of the pot to see if the type of metal is indicated there. If you're not sure, ask the cook in your house.)

PROCEDURE

1   Divide the cabbage evenly between the 2 aluminum pots. Cut the apple into quarters and remove the core. Cut the apple into chunks and add them to one of the pots. Add just enough water to cover the bottom of each pot (¼ to ½ cup).

2   Cook the cabbage over low heat for about 20 minutes, stirring occasionally.

OBSERVATIONS

Which cooked cabbage is redder? Which one contained acid? How do your findings support the idea that small amounts of aluminum combine with water to form aluminum hydroxide, a base? What did the apple do to this base?

You can also prepare your indicator from cooked cabbage but, of course, you can't cook it in an aluminum pot. Put raw grated cabbage in a stainless steel, porcelain, or glass pot and cover with water. Cook over low heat for 3 or 4 minutes, until it boils. Then drain off the liquid. The cooked cabbage and the indicator will be a darker red than the uncooked indicator. Compare indicators to see which one you prefer using.

Mixed with salt, pepper, and butter, the cooked cabbage goes well with pot roast. Save your red cabbage indicator in the refrigerator, where it will keep for a few days without spoiling. Keep the indicator in a closed jar, because it has a strong odor.

OPTICALLY ACTIVE SYRUPS

One characteristic of a true solution is that it is perfectly clear when you shine a light through it. You cannot see the beam traveling through the solution when you look at it sideways, but you can see what it illuminates when it comes out the other side.

If you shine a special kind of light, called *polarized light*, through a syrup, a very concentrated sugar solution, you may see an interesting phenomenon. But first, let me shine some light on the nature of light. This involves thinking in three dimensions.

Light is a form of energy that travels in waves. Watch some water waves. If you throw a pebble into a quiet pond you'll see the ripples of water spread away from the impact that is the energy source that propagates the wave. The departing wave has a crest and a trough. If you looked at the wave sideways you'd see that the high point and low point of the wave are at right angles to the plane of the direction the wave is traveling, called the axis of propagation. A cork on a wave bobs up and down but is not carried along with the wave. (Can you think of a way to test this out?) The height of a water wave is measured at a right angle to the surface of the water when there are no waves. This diagram shows the parts of a wave and how it moves:

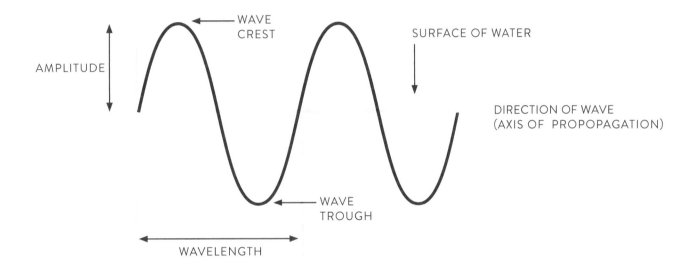

Light is a little more complicated than water waves because the waves are not just traveling in one horizontal plane but in many planes all at right angles to the axis of propagation, which is the line or direction in which the waves are traveling. You can think of the up-and-down motion of the wave as a vibration.

What happens if you put a "gate" in front of ordinary light so that all the light waves are blocked except for those that are vibrating in only one plane? The light that emerges on the other side of the gate is polarized. The diagram on page 26 shows how such a gate stops all light that isn't vibrating in a vertical plane.

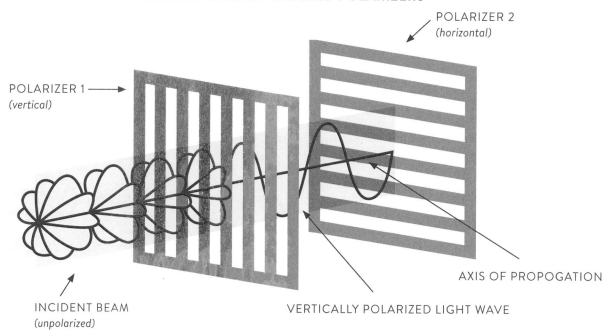

LIGHT PASSING THROUGH CROSSED POLARIZERS

POLARIZER 2
(horizontal)

POLARIZER 1
(vertical)

AXIS OF PROPOGATION

INCIDENT BEAM
(unpolarized)

VERTICALLY POLARIZED LIGHT WAVE

The lenses in polarized sunglasses are an example of this kind of gate. Glare, light that is bouncing off surfaces on a sunny day, is for the most part horizontally polarized. So the lenses in polarized sunglasses are positioned vertically to block horizontally polarized light and keep glare from reaching your eyes. However, if you tilt your head, when you look at glare, some light may get through.

See for yourself: Suppose the light that emerges from one polarized sunglass lens is traveling in a vertical plane. If another lens is placed on top of the first and it is rotated so that it only allows light traveling in a horizontal plane to pass through, then the incoming light will be completely blocked. Try it. Place one polarized lens on top of another and rotate one lens until the light is completely blocked. As you rotate the top lens, varying amounts of light will appear.

Certain sugar solutions are *optically active*. This means that they have the ability to rotate polarized light. The next experiment is not a recipe but it shows pancake syrup in a new light.

MATERIALS & EQUIPMENT

- various syrups in clear containers (maple, pancake, and corn syrups; diluted molasses; the sugar solution you made from rock candy)

- a lens from a pair of polarized sunglasses. You can buy inexpensive plastic polarized sunglasses at dollar stores. (Make sure you get permission before you sacrifice a pair of sunglasses to science.)

- a blank white computer screen (like a blank Word document). The light that comes from your screen is a source of polarized white light.

- small, clear glasses to hold samples of syrup

PROCEDURE

1   First, see how the light from your computer is polarized. Hold one sunglass lens in front of you so that you see the light from the screen. Slowly rotate the lens. When your lens is perpendicular to the plane of the polarized light coming from the screen, all the light will be blocked and the lens will be black.

2   Pour a sample of syrup into a small, clear glass. Hold the glass in front of the screen. Look at the syrup through the polarized lens. As you slowly rotate it you will see a series of colors that are a progression through the rainbow: red, orange, yellow, green, blue, indigo, violet. ("Roy G. Biv" is an outstanding mnemonic, or phrase to help you remember the order of the colors, going from the longest wavelengths to the shortest.) All white

light is made up of all the colors of the rainbow. Each color has a different wavelength going from red (the longest) to violet (the shortest).

3   If you want to see the difference with unpolarized light, hold a glass with a syrup sample up to sunlight. Rotate one sunglass lens as you look through it. You will not see the color progression.

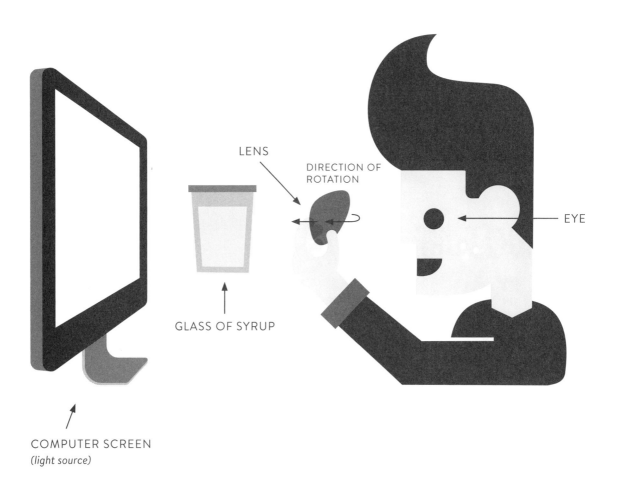

LENS

DIRECTION OF ROTATION

EYE

GLASS OF SYRUP

COMPUTER SCREEN
(light source)

OBSERVATIONS

When polarized white light passes through the syrup, each colored wave in the white light is rotated by a slightly different amount. As you turn the polarized lens in front of the syrup bottle, it filters out the separate waves so you see a sequence of colors. The concepts of polarized light and optical activity are quite complicated, and you might want to read more about them in an optics book.

Biochemists use a device called a *polarimeter* to measure how optically active a sugar solution is. *Glucose*, one of the most important sugars we eat, is also called *dextrose* because it rotates polarized light to the right ("dextro" means "right") or clockwise. *Fructose*, another kind of simple sugar, often found in fruit, is sometimes called *levulose* because it rotates polarized light to the left or counterclockwise. The optical activity of sugars is an important method in biochemistry for identifying sugars and understanding the structure of sugar molecules. The way a sugar solution acts in polarized light is directly related to the structure of its molecules.

Unlike the syrup you made for rock candy, the syrups you buy for pancakes are designed to remain crystal free. Syrups that contain different kinds of sugars will not form crystals easily because the different sugar molecules don't fit together.

SUSPENSIONS, COLLOIDS, AND EMULSIONS

Matter is found in all kinds of mixtures, including mixtures with water. A solution is one kind of mixture, but there are others. Figuring out all the different parts of mixtures is a challenge for scientists.

Water is called the universal solvent because more things dissolve in water than any other liquid. But not everything dissolves in it. Some water mixtures, such as mud, contain particles that are heavy enough to settle on the bottom

after being stirred up. This kind of mixture is called a *suspension* because the material is suspended only temporarily in the liquid. You can separate the liquid from the large solid particles in a suspension by letting the particles settle and then by pouring off the liquid. This method of separation is called *decanting*. If a suspension contains very small particles, it may take days or weeks to settle. Decanting either isn't practical or won't work with these mixtures. Instead, you can separate the particles by pouring the mixture through a strainer or filter. Filtration can also be used to determine the size of the suspended particles.

Do the next experiment to discover more about suspensions and the way they are handled by scientists.

BORSCHT COCKTAIL
SEPARATING SUSPENDED PARTICLES

A *puree* is a suspension of food particles in a liquid. Purees are made with food processors or blenders or by pushing soft food through a strainer. Usually the pureed food particles are so small that they take a long time to settle. Pea soup, tomato sauce, and applesauce are examples of purees. Jarred beet soup, or borscht, is good for beginning a study of suspensions, involving a beet puree.

MATERIALS & EQUIPMENT

- a jar of borscht (any size)
- 1 tablespoon sour cream
- a watch with a second hand
- a strainer
- 2 glass jars
- some coffee filters
- a large spoon
- a wire whisk or an eggbeater

PROCEDURE 1

1   Shake the jar of borscht. Use the watch to time how long it takes for the beet particles to settle on the bottom. Do some beet particles stay suspended longer than others? Which ones stay suspended longer?

2   Pour (decant) about a cup of the settled liquid through a strainer into a glass jar.

OBSERVATIONS

Are any beet particles caught by the strainer? What is the size of particles that pass through the strainer? Are they smaller or larger than the holes in the strainer?

PROCEDURE 2

1   Rinse out the strainer. Put a coffee filter in the bottom of the strainer and then place the strainer over the top of the second glass jar.

2   Pour the liquid you have just strained from the first glass jar through the filter paper and let the mixture drip through.

OBSERVATIONS

What evidence do you have that the filter paper has holes even though you can't see them? Are there any beet particles on the filter paper? Are these particles smaller or larger than the holes in the filter paper?

Taste the liquid that you have just filtered. Is there sugar in borscht? How can you tell? (Confirm your observations by reading the list of ingredients on the label.) What can you say about the size of sugar particles compared to the size of the (too small to see) holes in the filter paper?

PROCEDURE 3

1 Remove the filter paper from the strainer, but keep the strainer on top of the glass jar. Take 2 large spoonfuls of beets from the bottom of the jar of borscht. Push them through the strainer with a spoon into the liquid in the glass jar. Be sure to scrape the beets off the outside of the strainer. You can use some of the liquid from the jar you are straining into to wash the pureed beets through the strainer. Pour it into another container so you can catch everything in the glass jar.

2 Stir or shake the pureed beets into the liquid.

OBSERVATIONS

How long does it take these particles to settle? Do they all settle eventually? How does the settling time compare with the time for the pieces of beet before they were pureed? (If you find it difficult to see the beets, work in front of a strong light.)

From the results of your experiment, can you explain how settling rates and filtering can be used to find the size of particles? Can you think of how these procedures can be used to identify different substances as well as to separate them? Can you design an experiment to test the speeds on a blender or the blades on a food processor by creating purees with coarser and finer particles?

You can make a delicious cold soup with your experiment. Chill the pureed mixture. Beat in about a tablespoon of sour cream with a whisk or an eggbeater.

LIQUID FOOD AND THE TYNDALL EFFECT

Solutions and suspensions are both mixtures with two phases. One phase, the solvent, can be thought of as *continuous*. That is, all the particles are in contact with one another. The second phase, the solute, can be thought of as *discontinuous*. The solute particles are separated from one another by the solvent. The main difference between true solutions and suspensions is the size of the particles of the solute phase. In a solution, solute particles are approximately the size of single molecules. In a suspension, the particles are made up of countless numbers of molecules and are large enough to be filterable.

A *colloid* is a third kind of mixture with these two phases. The suspended particles in a colloid are larger than single molecules but small enough to remain in suspension permanently and be homogeneous. It is hard to tell the difference between a

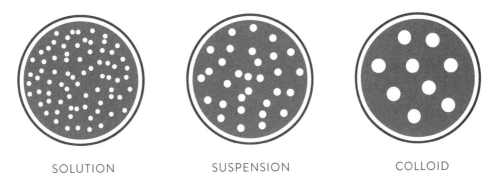

SOLUTION SUSPENSION COLLOID

colloid and a solution just by looking at them. There is, however, a simple test that does tell the difference. All you need is a clear glass and a flashlight.

If you pass a beam of light through a colloid and you look at the beam from the side, you can see the beam. This is because the particles in a colloid are large enough to act as tiny mirrors and reflect light. This light-scattering ability is called the *Tyndall effect*. You can see the Tyndall effect in a beam of sunlight in a dusty room or from car headlights on a foggy night. Fog and dust particles are large enough to reflect light, while air molecules are too small.

You can also see the Tyndall effect in liquids we drink. Pour a small sample of a liquid into a clear glass. Hold the glass against a dark background and shine a flashlight beam through it. (A pen flashlight works especially well.) Look at the beam from the side. If you can see the beam as it passes through, the liquid is a colloid. If you can't see the beam from the side, the liquid is a solution.

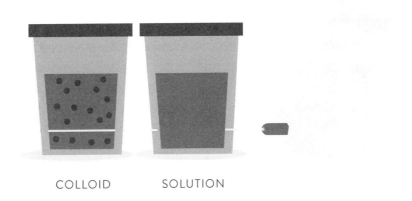

COLLOID   SOLUTION

Which of the following liquids are colloids and which are solutions? Tea, cranberry juice, syrup (colorless), orange drink (not juice), coffee, salt water, Jell-O, Kool-Aid, consommé, vinegar (distilled), egg white, cider.

Protoplasm, the living material of all cells, is a complicated colloid. What would you expect if you shone a beam of light through a cell?

SALAD DRESSING
A LIQUID SUSPENDED IN A LIQUID

If you shake oil and water together and then let them stand, they will separate into two layers. Liquids that do not form solutions are said to be *immiscible*.

Classic French salad dressing (or vinaigrette) is a mixture of oil and vinegar and seasoning. Vinegar is a water-based substance (an acid) and is immiscible with oil. In order for all the flavors of the dressing to be evenly spread through a salad, it must be thoroughly mixed. A vinaigrette is usually given a number of hard shakes and immediately poured on a salad before the two liquids have a chance to separate.

This experiment is designed to answer the question: Does the size of the droplets of two immiscible liquids affect the rate of separation into layers?

MATERIALS & EQUIPMENT

- ⅓ cup vinegar
- ½ teaspoon salt
- 1 cup salad oil (olive, vegetable, or safflower)
- measuring cups and spoons
- ¼ teaspoon pepper
- ¼ teaspoon garlic powder
- watch or clock with a second hand
- a small bowl
- a 2-cup jar with a tight screw-on cover
- ¼ teaspoon paprika
- an eggbeater or electric mixer
- a magnifying glass

PROCEDURE 1

1 Put the vinegar in the jar and add the salt, pepper, garlic powder, and paprika. Screw the lid on tight and shake.

2 Pour in the salad oil and let the mixture stand for a few minutes.

OBSERVATIONS

Where does the oil go? Which do you think would be heavier, a cup of water or a cup of oil? Can you think of a way to check your guess?

PROCEDURE 2

1   Cover the jar and shake about 10 times. Use the watch to see how long it takes for the mixture to separate. Can you see which is the continuous phase and which is the discontinuous?

2   Shake the jar hard about 20 times. Does the dressing take more or less time to separate? Look for droplets of vinegar suspended in the oil.

3   Shake the jar different numbers of times and examine the size of the droplets immediately after shaking. When does the dressing have the smallest droplets?

4   Put the mixture in a small bowl and beat hard for about 4 minutes with an eggbeater or electric mixer. Quickly pour the dressing back into the jar. Examine the droplets with a magnifying glass. How long does the dressing take to separate into two layers? What did shaking and beating do to the size of the droplets?

You can use the French dressing over a tossed green salad. Mix well and use just enough to coat the leaves lightly.

EMULSIONS

If milk, fresh from a cow, is allowed to stand, the fat rises to the top as cream. When milk is homogenized, it is forced through tiny holes in a screen. This breaks up the butterfat into very tiny droplets. Why doesn't the butterfat separate from milk when it is homogenized?

A suspension of two immiscible liquids that doesn't separate on standing is called an *emulsion*. The word "emulsion" comes from a Latin word that means "to milk out." Emulsions have a milky or cloudy appearance. Cream is an emulsion in which droplets of butterfat are suspended in a water-based continuous phase. The water part of milk or cream contains some milk proteins and sugar. If you put heavy cream in a jar with a tight cover and shake hard for a few minutes, you will produce the opposite result from the French dressing. When you make French dressing, shaking causes the discontinuous phase (the vinegar) to break up into tiny droplets and disperse throughout the continuous phase (the oil). If you shake heavy cream, you cause the tiny droplets of butterfat (the discontinuous phase) to come in contact with one another. This will be explored in the next chapter when you make butter.

MAYONNAISE

A STABILIZED EMULSION

When oil and vinegar in French dressing separate, the vinegar droplets grow larger and larger, and the oil droplets grow larger and larger. The large oil droplets float to the surface of the vinegar. If, however, you add a certain third substance to a mixture of oil and vinegar, you can stabilize the mixture and prevent the separation. The result is a stable emulsion of two immiscible liquids, and the substance that keeps the two liquids from separating is called an *emulsifying agent.*

One example of an emulsifying agent is soap. When you wash greasy dishes, hot water turns the grease into oil. One end of a soap molecule attaches to the grease and the other end is soluble in water. Each grease droplet is held in suspension in the water by countless soap molecules. The emulsified grease is easily washed down the drain. Try washing greasy dishes without soap, first in cold water and then in hot water, to see how emulsifying by soap works. Can you get the dishes clean?

Mayonnaise is an emulsion of oil in vinegar. Vinegar is an acid in water (a solution). In the process of making mayonnaise, you disperse five parts oil into only one part water. The vinegar

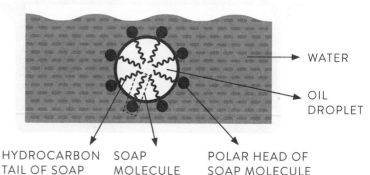

WATER

OIL DROPLET

HYDROCARBON TAIL OF SOAP   SOAP MOLECULE   POLAR HEAD OF SOAP MOLECULE forms a thin coating around the oil droplets. The emulsifying agent is egg yolks. Making mayonnaise is a real challenge to many who pride themselves on being good cooks, but it is not difficult to make if you understand what is happening as the emulsion forms.

MATERIALS & EQUIPMENT

- 2 egg yolks (see page 238 for how to separate eggs)

- ½ teaspoon prepared (not powdered, dry) mustard

- ½ teaspoon salt

- 3 tablespoons vinegar

- 1 cup salad oil (olive, vegetable, or safflower)

- measuring cups and spoons

- a small bowl

- an electric mixer or a friend and an eggbeater

PROCEDURE

Before you start, have all the ingredients at room temperature. Cold oil doesn't flow as quickly as warmer oil, and cold egg yolks will not emulsify as much oil as warmer egg yolks. (Can you think of experiments to check these ideas out?)

1   Put the egg yolks, mustard, salt, and 1 teaspoon of the vinegar in the bowl and beat at a medium speed until the egg yolks are lemon-colored. The egg yolks are now thoroughly mixed with the water in the vinegar and are ready to receive the oil.

2   Add the oil very slowly, bit by bit, while beating continuously. If you do not

have an electric mixer, you can make the emulsion by hand with a friend. One of you does the beating with an eggbeater while the other adds the oil.

OBSERVATIONS

The idea in making mayonnaise is to spread tiny droplets of oil evenly through the egg yolks. Egg yolk coats these droplets as they form and prevents them from coming together and developing a separate layer. If you add the oil too fast or too much oil at one time, the droplets will come together before they can be forced into the egg yolks and the mayonnaise will "curdle" or separate. If this happens, you can correct the situation with a fresh egg yolk by adding the curdled mayonnaise to the yolk rather than the other way around.

You can tell when the emulsion has formed because the mixture gets thick. This usually happens after about ⅓ cup of oil has been added.

Once the emulsion has formed, you can add the oil slightly faster, until the full cup has been beaten in to the yolks. If the mixture gets too thick, add a teaspoon of the vinegar. Beat in the remaining vinegar at the end.

Homemade mayonnaise is thick, yellow, and glistening. It spoils easily and should be stored in the refrigerator. Cover it so a skin doesn't form on top.

Several cookbooks make the claim that mayonnaise is difficult to make on a rainy day or when a thunderstorm is threatening. But mayonnaise is made commercially on every working day regardless of the weather. You might want to do some experiments to check this out.

STRAWBERRY BOMBE
A FROZEN EMULSION

Ice cream, bombes, and other frozen desserts contain water and cream. Separation of the fat in ice cream is not a problem because the fat droplets are very small. In frozen desserts the challenge is to keep the water droplets small. Large water droplets form large ice crystals and give the dessert a grainy texture. As long as the ice crystals are tiny, the dessert will be smooth.

Suppose an emulsifying agent that attracts water is an ingredient in a frozen dessert. Do you think it can keep large ice crystals from forming, just as egg yolks keep large oil droplets from forming in mayonnaise? Discover the answer by making the strawberry bombe in the next experiment.

MATERIALS & EQUIPMENT

- 1 teaspoon unflavored gelatin

- 4½ tablespoons cold water

- 1½ tablespoons boiling water

- 2 cups heavy or whipping cream, defrosted

- a spoon

- a pen and labels

- an electric mixer or eggbeater

Continued . . .

- 1 (9- or 10-ounce) package frozen strawberries, defrosted
- 1 cup sugar
- 2 teaspoons lemon juice
- measuring cups and spoons
- a small dish or cup
- 3 small bowls
- a rubber spatula
- 2 (1-pint) containers (plastic ice cream containers are good)

PROCEDURE

1   Put the gelatin in the small dish or cup and add 1½ tablespoons of the cold water.

2   Does the gelatin attract water? How can you tell? You may have to wait a few minutes before you can answer these questions.

3   Put the strawberries in one of the bowls and add the sugar and lemon juice. Mix well and then pour half the strawberry mixture into a second bowl.

4   When the gelatin has softened and absorbed all the cold water, add the boiling water and stir until all the gelatin dissolves. Add the gelatin mixture to one of the strawberry mixtures and stir well. Stir the remaining 3 tablespoons of cold water into the other strawberry mixture as a control. Label the bowls so you know which one contains the gelatin.

5   Refrigerate the strawberry mixtures until the gelatin starts to thicken. It should not be firm, only slightly gelled. Start checking after 15 minutes. When the gelatin mixture is ready, remove it from the refrigerator.

6   In the third bowl, whip the cream with a mixer or eggbeater until it stands

in soft peaks when you raise the beaters. Put half the whipped cream into each strawberry mixture.

7 Gently combine the strawberries and cream by using a rubber spatula to bring the mixture from the bottom of the bowl to the top. Repeat this motion again and again, until the whipped cream and strawberries are well mixed. (This is what is known as "folding" two ingredients together.)

8 Pour one strawberry-and-cream mixture into each pint container. Be sure to label the one containing the gelatin. Put the containers into the freezer for about 12 hours. When the desserts are frozen, taste them.

OBSERVATIONS

Is there a difference in texture between the dessert containing gelatin and the one without?

Let a few tablespoons of each dessert thaw and then refreeze them. Which dessert has a grainier texture? What do you think the gelatin does in a strawberry bombe?

CONSOMMÉ

CLARIFICATION BY FLOCCULATION

Canned broths and bouillon cubes are staple foods in almost every kitchen. But true chefs pride themselves on their "stockpots," the broths they create with leftovers from daily food preparation. It takes time to create a broth—hours of simmering on the stove. Broths are cloudy with all kinds of suspended particles. In other words, they are complicated suspensions and colloids with many kinds of particles in the discontinuous phase. A true bouillon or consommé is clear and sparkling. The word *bouillon* comes from the French word for "boil." The word *consommé* comes from a word that means the "highest." In the next experiment, you will create your own broth and clarify it—that is, remove the particles—to make consommé. The project takes two days to complete. It will give you a real appreciation for homemade stock, and also for inexpensive, easy-to-use canned consommés and bouillon cubes. It will also show you a method for removing particles that is often used in many chemical industries.

MATERIALS & EQUIPMENT

- 1 pound lean beef, sliced
- 2 onions, peeled
- 2 stalks celery with leaves
- 2 leeks, washed
- a 4-quart soup pot

- about 1 pound beef bones (ask the butcher at your supermarket)
- water
- 2 carrots, peeled
- 2 teaspoons salt
- 6 sprigs fresh parsley
- ¼ teaspoon dried thyme
- a slotted spoon
- a 2-quart bowl or container
- a knife

PROCEDURE

1   Put the meat and bones in the soup pot and add enough cold water to fill the pot about three-quarters full. Set the pot on the stove over low to medium heat. As the liquid starts to simmer, a scum will rise to the surface. Skim it off with a slotted spoon until it stops forming. This will take about 5 minutes. It is important not to let the soup boil violently, as the scum will be returned to the broth and make it even cloudier.

2   Add the rest of the ingredients and let the mixture simmer, uncovered, for at least 4 hours. The liquid will be reduced by about half.

3   Remove all the solid ingredients from the broth using the slotted spoon. They are good to eat. Pour the broth into a bowl or container. Notice that the liquid fat rises to the surface. Refrigerate, uncovered, overnight.

4   The next day the fat will be a hard, whitish layer on top of the broth. Remove it by cutting around the edge with a knife to separate it from the wall of the bowl or container. The whole layer of fat can be lifted out in one piece. Fish out any remaining pieces of fat with a slotted spoon. Notice how cloudy the broth is. You're going to get rid of the cloudiness with an almost-magical procedure using egg whites. This is the clarification procedure.

MATERIALS & EQUIPMENT

- 2 egg whites
- ½ of the cold stock (about 1 quart)
- 2 eggshells, crushed
- a small bowl

- a wire whisk
- a 2-quart saucepan
- a colander
- cheesecloth (from the supermarket or hardware store)

- a large bowl
- a spoon
- a ladle

PROCEDURE

1   Beat the egg whites slightly with a wire whisk in a small bowl. Put 1 quart of your stock in a saucepan and beat in the egg whites with the whisk. Add the crushed eggshells. Place the saucepan over low heat and slowly, without stirring, let the soup come to a simmer so that it is barely moving. **Do not let the soup boil, or the egg white will break up and fail to clarify the soup.** The egg white and shells float to the surface of the soup, forming a "raft" that is strengthened by the eggshell pieces. The egg white is *coagulating* (more on this in chapter 5, "Proteins") and becoming firm due to the heat. Amazingly it acts like a magnet for some of the larger particles floating in the broth. This process of drawing out impurities by collecting them in bunches is called *flocculation*. (Stump your folks at the dinner table with that word tonight.) Carefully simmer your broth for about 15 minutes. Remove from the heat and allow it to cool, undisturbed, for about an hour.

2   Line the colander with 8 layers of wet and wrung-out cheesecloth. Set it above the large bowl. Gently push the raft to one side with a spoon and carefully ladle the broth into the cheesecloth, which will filter out any egg white and eggshell particles.

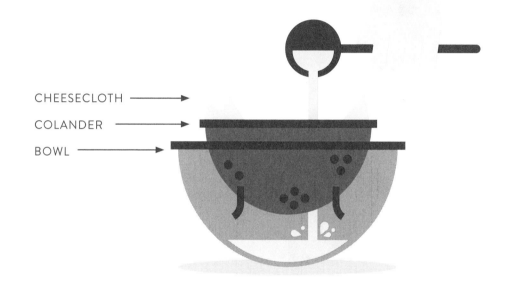

CHEESECLOTH ⟶

COLANDER ⟶

BOWL ⟶

OBSERVATIONS

Compare the clarified broth with the original broth. If you made a mistake and boiled the egg white mixture, you can chill it and try the process again with fresh egg whites. You can clarify the other half of the broth or not, as you wish. It is perfectly good to eat unclarified.

Taste your consommé. If it is not as strong as you might like, add a bouillon cube or two. You can add cooked noodles or vegetables or meat to create any number of soups from your consommé. Eat and enjoy.

4

CARBOHYDRATES AND FATS

Solutions, suspensions, and emulsions are all mixtures that can be separated and purified into simpler substances. One question that challenged scientists was: What are the simplest substances of all? It turns out that there are only two kinds of pure substances on earth: *compounds* and *elements*.

Elements are the simplest kinds of pure matter. Ninety-eight elements have been identified in the earth's atmosphere and crust and a number of others have been made in laboratories. The most common elements found in food (and that also make up your body) are carbon, hydrogen, oxygen, and nitrogen. Living things also contain sulfur, phosphorus, iron, magnesium, sodium, potassium, and chlorine, to name a few.

It took a long time to discover all the elements. This is because elements combine to form compounds, and it was hard to tell whether a pure substance was an element or if it was a compound. Water is a good example. Water is an extremely stable compound, and it takes enormous amounts of energy to break it up into its elements. So for hundreds of years, people thought that water was an element. It was a great scientific breakthrough when water was found to be a compound made of hydrogen and oxygen, two gases known to be elements.

Elements combine to form compounds very differently from the way substances combine to form mixtures. The properties of the components of mixtures don't change as a result of being part of a mixture. But most compounds have very different properties from the elements that are its components. (Think how water is different from oxygen and hydrogen. Hydrogen is an explosive gas. Oxygen is also a gas, and it supports burning and life. Water is a liquid at ordinary temperatures and neither burns nor supports burning.) Compounds are also made of fixed amounts of combined elements. Any amounts of hydrogen and oxygen gases can be mixed together, but water forms from two parts of hydrogen and one part of oxygen. Any extra hydrogen or oxygen present from the original mixture will be left over after water has formed.

Sugars and starches are compounds that are important kinds of food. They are made of only three elements—carbon, hydrogen, and oxygen. When sugars and starches are broken down into these elements, there are two atoms of hydrogen and one of oxygen for every atom of carbon. Two atoms of hydrogen and one atom of oxygen are the same as a molecule of water. For this reason, sugars and starches were called *carbohydrates*, which means "watered carbon." This chapter investigates some of the properties of this interesting group of compounds.

Simple sugars are manufactured by green plants through a process called *photosynthesis*. Carbon dioxide in the air combines with water to form a six-carbon molecule called *glucose*. It takes energy, which comes from the sun, to make this molecule. One very important job of a food is to provide energy to living things, to be a fuel for all life functions. The most direct source of this energy is glucose. So green plants are at the very bottom of the food chain, since they make their own food. Plants that are not green and all animal life could not survive without green plants.

SYRUPS

SOLUTIONS THAT DON'T CRYSTALLIZE

One property of sugar is that it dissolves in water. If it didn't, you couldn't make rock candy. Actually, making rock candy involves recovering solute crystals from solution, not dissolving them. Corn syrup, molasses, maple syrup, and honey are all examples of sugar solutions. Do the next experiment to see if you can recover sugar crystals from these solutions.

Pour a small amount of each kind of syrup into small shallow dishes and let them stand uncovered for several days. In some cases no crystals will form and you will be left with a thick, sticky material coating the dish. Scientists are always looking for testable questions, ones that can be answered by experimenting. Answering the question "Why don't sugar crystals form from such syrups?" could lead to other testable questions.

Perhaps the syrups are not reaching the supersaturated condition necessary for crystallization to occur. Does syrup absorb water from the air even while water is evaporating from its surface so that most of the sugar remains in solution?

To test this idea, make a supersaturated sugar solution as for rock candy (see chapter 2, pages 9–12). Divide the solution between two dishes. Leave one dish exposed to the air and cover the other with a cake cover or large glass bowl. Before you cover the second dish, sprinkle some calcium chloride on the table around it. Calcium chloride absorbs moisture from the air and will keep the air above the dish dry. You can get calcium chloride in hobby shops or on the internet. It can also be found in little bags in some vitamin bottles.

Do crystals form more slowly from solutions containing several solutes than from a solution containing only one solute?

MATERIALS & EQUIPMENT

- 1½ cups water
- 2 cups sugar
- 7½ tablespoons white corn syrup
- ½ teaspoon cream of tartar
- a saucepan with a cover

- a wooden spoon
- a candy thermometer
- 3 small foil dishes
- magnifying glass

PROCEDURE

1 Put ½ cup of the water, ⅔ cup of the sugar, 2½ tablespoons of the corn syrup, and ¼ teaspoon of the cream of tartar into the saucepan and stir over medium heat until dissolved. When the mixture starts to boil, cover it briefly so that the steam washes all the sugar crystallized on the side of the saucepan back into the solution.

2 Uncover the saucepan and put in the candy thermometer. Continue to boil, without stirring, until the temperature reaches 290°F (143°C). Carefully pour the syrup into a foil dish.

3 & 4 Make two more batches of syrup with new ingredients and these small variations: In the second batch, leave out the cream of tartar. In the third batch, use the cream of tartar but heat the mixture only until all the sugar is dissolved. As the solutions cook, you can tell when crystals have formed because the solution becomes cloudy. Close examination with a magnifying glass will reveal thousands of tiny, needle-like crystals.

OBSERVATIONS

Where do crystals form? They should form in two of the syrup batches, while one should remain clear.

There are a number of different kinds of sugars. All are sweet and they all dissolve in water. Some sugars contain only five or six carbon atoms per molecule. These are called simple sugars, and they include *glucose* (sometimes called dextrose) from beets, *fructose* from fruit, and *lactose* from milk. Table sugar is called *sucrose*. It is not a simple sugar because each sucrose molecule is a two-molecule chain of one fructose molecule and one glucose molecule linked together.

When a sucrose solution is heated to a high temperature, it begins to break down into glucose and fructose. This breakdown is speeded up with the addition of an acid such as cream of tartar. The result is a syrup containing a mixture of three sugar solutes—glucose, fructose, and sucrose. Crystals will not form in such a mixture because a crystal is the result of a regular arrangement of identical molecules. When there are several different kinds of molecules in a solution, similar molecules have a harder time getting together.

The syrups you have made can be poured over ice cream or popcorn.

HYGROSCOPIC COOKIES

Ever notice how cookies lose their crispness when they've been exposed to air for a while? Cookie manufacturers have. That's why they seal their products in packages that keep them from being exposed to water vapor in the air. The ingredient in cookies that is chiefly responsible for absorbing moisture is sugar. Such a substance is described as *hygroscopic*, which means "wet looking."

Is one kind of sugar more hygroscopic than another? The next experiment compares cookies made with granulated sucrose and those made with honey. Taste honey and sugar. Which is sweeter?

MATERIALS & EQUIPMENT

- 2 cups flour

- 1 teaspoon baking powder

- ½ teaspoon salt

- 1 stick (½ cup) unsalted butter, softened

- ½ cup sugar

- 1 egg

- 2 tablespoons water

- ½ teaspoon lemon juice

- ¼ cup honey

- measuring cups and spoons

- a flour sifter

- a fork

- 4 small bowls

- an electric mixer or eggbeater

- waxed paper

- greased cookie sheets

- a metal spatula

- wire cooling racks

PROCEDURE

1 Preheat the oven to 400°F (204°C). Sift the flour onto waxed paper. Use a roomy work space and keep the flour on the waxed paper. Measure out 1 cup of the sifted flour and resift it together with ½ teaspoon of the baking powder and ¼ teaspoon of the salt into a bowl.

2 Resift the second cup of flour with the remaining ½ teaspoon baking powder and ¼ teaspoon salt into a second bowl. Set the dry ingredients aside.

3 Put ½ stick of the softened butter into a third bowl. Beat until creamy with an electric mixer or eggbeater. Add the sugar to the butter and continue beating until thoroughly mixed.

4 Beat the egg with a fork in a measuring cup. Put half the egg into the butter-sugar mixture. Then add one of the bowls of dry ingredients, as well as the water and lemon juice, to the butter-sugar mixture. Beat until smooth.

5 Now prepare the batter with honey: Put the remaining ½ stick softened butter in a fourth bowl and beat until creamy. Beat in the honey. Add the other half of the egg and the second bowl of dry ingredients to the butter-honey mixture. You do not need to put in lemon juice as honey already contains an acid. Mix until well blended.

6 Drop small spoonfuls of the batter onto greased cookie sheets, leaving about 2 inches between the cookies. Bake until brown around the edges, about 7 minutes. Be sure to keep track of which cookies contain sugar and which contain honey.

7 Let the cookies cool for a few minutes on the sheets before moving them to a wire rack with a metal spatula. When they are completely cool, store the cookies in airtight containers.

OBSERVATIONS

When they are cool, eat a sugar cookie and a honey cookie. Are they about the same crispness? Are they the same color? Which is browner? Leave one of each kind of cookie exposed to the air. Take a bite of each every few hours. Which cookie loses its crispness more quickly? If you wanted to make a cake that would stay moist for a long time, what sweetener might you use?

STARCHES

Sucrose is a two-molecule chain of simple sugars. A starch molecule is made of long chains of simple sugar molecules. Plants make starch molecules as a way of storing sugar because it can be easily converted back to sugar when needed for energy and as a structural part of the plant in the form of *cellulose*. If you have any doubt that starch is made of sugar, an experiment using a chemical made by your own body can give you the answer. When you digest starches, your body breaks them down into sugars, which you use for energy. If you don't need the sugar right away, the starch can be stored in your liver. Or it can be converted to fat and stored all over your body.

MATERIALS & EQUIPMENT

• a soda cracker, saltine, or other plain flour cracker

• your taste buds

PROCEDURE

A soda cracker is made of flour (a starch), water, and baking powder. It contains no sugar. Check the ingredients listed on the box to make sure. Chew a soda cracker well and hold it in your mouth, without swallowing, for 5 minutes.

OBSERVATIONS

Does the taste of the soda cracker change? There is a special chemical in your saliva that breaks the links in the starch chains so that sugar molecules are released. You should be able to taste this change.

Compare some of the properties of starches and sugars. How is the taste different? Try putting different starches in water. In addition to flour, common starches include arrowroot starch, cornstarch, and potato starch. Which dissolves most easily? In general, small molecules dissolve more easily than larger molecules. Sugar dissolves more easily than starch.

Like sugar, starches also absorb water. When starches are heated with water, they swell. This property, called *gelatinization*, makes them very useful as thickeners for sauces and gravies.

Many different foods contain starch. There is a simple chemical test for starch. Put a few drops of iodine solution (called tincture of iodine, available in most drugstores) on the food. If starch is present, the iodine changes from reddish-brown to a blue-black. **Don't eat any food on which you put iodine! Iodine is poisonous.**

TAPIOCA

Tapioca is a starch that comes from the root of a Brazilian cassava plant. Cassava flour is rolled into little balls, which are sold as dried "pearls." Tapioca pearls are used to make thick puddings.

Put a drop of iodine on a tapioca pearl. Does it give a positive starch test? Discard the pearl you tested. Take ¼ cup of tapioca pearls and put them in ¾ cup of water. Let them soak for 12 hours. How does the size of the soaked tapioca compare with dried pearls? How is this evidence that starches swell with water?

You can make tapioca pudding with the soaked pearls.

TAPIOCA PUDDING RECIPE

MATERIALS & EQUIPMENT

- ¼ cup tapioca pearls, soaked in ¾ cup water
- ¼ teaspoon salt
- 2½ cups milk
- water
- ½ cup sugar
- 2 eggs
- 1 teaspoon vanilla extract
- a small bowl
- a double boiler
- an eggbeater
- a wooden spoon
- plastic wrap
- 4 dessert cups
- measuring cups and spoons

PROCEDURE

1. Test a small sample of milk, salt, eggs, sugar, and vanilla for starch. **Don't use any of the ingredients you have tested when you are preparing the pudding.** Is starch present in any of these ingredients?

2. Put the soaked pearls in the top of a double boiler with the milk and salt. Fill the bottom of the double boiler about three-quarters full with water and set over medium heat. Cook the tapioca mixture, uncovered, over boiling water for about an hour, stirring occasionally with a wooden spoon.

3   After the hour is up, beat the eggs with the sugar in a small bowl. Mix a few spoonfuls of the hot tapioca mixture into the egg-sugar mixture. This will warm up the eggs slowly. If you were to put the eggs directly into the hot tapioca mixture, they would cook and you'd have scrambled eggs in your tapioca.

4   Add the warmed egg-sugar mixture to the tapioca in the pot. Cook for about 3 minutes more.

5   Remove the double boiler from the stove. Remove the top pot and set aside to cool for 15 minutes. Then mix in the vanilla. Divide the pudding among four dessert dishes, cover with plastic wrap, and chill.

6   Test part of the pudding (not a pearl) for starch. Then pick out a pearl from the pudding, wash it off, and test it for starch. What has happened to some of the starch that was in the tapioca pearls? What has this starch done to the liquid milk? Again, **don't eat** anything that has iodine on it.

GRAPE JELLY
HOW PECTIN ACTS

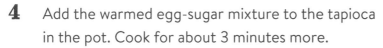

Pectin is a starch found in especially high amounts in green apples and the white underskin of citrus fruits. When pectin is cooked with sugar and acid, it swells to form a clear, thick jelly.

Pectin is prepared commercially and can be purchased in a package with an acid added but with no sugar. Is the added sugar necessary for the formation of a firm jelly? That's what the next experiment is designed to find out.

MATERIALS & EQUIPMENT

- 1 (6-ounce) can grape juice concentrate (thawed)

- 2 cups water

- 1 package Sure-Jell (commercially prepared pectin and acid)

- 3 cups sugar

- measuring cups and spoons

- a large saucepan

- a wooden spoon

- 4 (6-ounce) glasses or jelly jars

- a metal spoon

- melted paraffin for sealing off the jelly jars (not necessary if you will eat all the jelly within 2 weeks)

PROCEDURE

1   Put 3 ounces of the juice concentrate, 1 cup of the water, and ½ package (2½ tablespoons) of the Sure-Jell in a saucepan. Cook over high heat, stirring continuously, until bubbles form all around the edge.

2   Add 1 cup of the sugar all at once and stir. Bring the mixture to a rolling boil and allow it to boil, without stirring, for 1 minute.

3 Remove from the heat. Use a metal spoon to skim off the scum that rises to the surface. Pour the mixture into two glasses. If you plan to store the jelly, pour melted paraffin on top to seal it closed. Sealed jelly doesn't need to be refrigerated. Unsealed jelly does.

4 Make a second batch of jelly with the remaining juice concentrate, water, and Sure-Jell, and this time use 2 cups of sugar.

OBSERVATIONS

Which jelly is firmer? The softer jelly makes a good sauce for vanilla ice cream.

FATS AND OILS

Most of the compounds found in living organisms are made up of only a few of the ninety-eight naturally occurring elements. Carbon, hydrogen, and oxygen are found in a countless number of compounds. The differences in these compounds are due to the amounts of each element that are present and the way the atoms are arranged in the molecules.

Fats and oils, like carbohydrates, are a group of compounds made of only carbon, hydrogen, and oxygen. Fats and oils are produced by animals and plants as a method of storing food. Molecules of sugars and starches become fat or oil molecules as the atoms are rearranged. Stored fats and oils protect an organism against a time when food is scarce. Fats, starches, and sugars are needed for energy.

You can find out if a food contains fat or oil by rubbing it on a piece of brown paper bag. If the food contains a greasy substance, a translucent spot (an area that lets light through) will appear where you rubbed. Water in food will also produce a translucent spot, but a water spot disappears when the water dries. A fat or oil spot will not disappear.

Animal fats, such as butter or lard, are usually solids at room temperature, while vegetable fats are liquids. Vegetable oils can be made into solid fats in a laboratory by adding hydrogen gas under pressure. The terms *saturated* and *unsaturated* fats refer to the amount of hydrogen in a fat. Saturated fats contain more hydrogen than unsaturated or polyunsaturated. Saturated fats are usually solid, while unsaturated fats are oils. Margarine, which is advertised as being made from oil, contains some saturated fat. Hydrogen was added to make the fat solid.

Is there a difference between the ways these two kinds of fats act in the body? This is a question that has occupied scientists for years. When some people age, yellowish, fatty deposits of a substance called cholesterol form inside the arteries, leaving a narrower passage for blood to get through. This condition, called arteriosclerosis, can cause blood clots, which may block an artery and cause it to burst. It may also completely close an artery, cutting off the blood supply to a part of the body. If this happens in one of the arteries that nourishes the heart or brain, death can result. It appears that saturated fats in the diet may increase the amount of cholesterol in the body, and unsaturated fats may lower blood-cholesterol levels. For this reason, doctors suggest that older people cut down on the amounts of butter, cheese, and fatty meats in their diets. It is also behind the recent rulings to ban "trans" fats (which are saturated) from processed foods.

NUT BUTTER
PRESSING OUT OILS

Nuts contain oil, and oil burns easily with a steady flame. See for yourself by setting a Brazil nut on fire.

Stick the pointy triangular end of a can opener into the Brazil nut. Lay the can opener in a foil pan so the Brazil nut is held above the pan by the can opener. Ask a grown-up to hold a wooden match or a butane lighter to the end of the nut until the nut burns steadily. You can toast a marshmallow in the nut's flame.

Many vegetable oils are prepared by crushing olives, seeds, or nuts in presses. The oil is then separated from the nuts or seeds. In the next experiment, you will release the oil in nuts. Since it is difficult to separate the oil without the proper equipment, you will create a mixture of oil and nuts—a nut butter— that is good to eat.

MATERIALS & EQUIPMENT

- ½ to 1 cup shelled almonds, pecans, or walnuts

- a nut grinder or food processor

- a spatula

- 2 plastic bags

- a rolling pin

- a jar with a lid

PROCEDURE

You can use pecans or walnuts as they come out of the shell, but almonds should be white with their outer skins removed. This is done by putting shelled almonds into boiling water for a few minutes. Drain them and let them cool. They almost pop out of their skins if you hold them at the broad end and squeeze gently. You can buy skinless or "blanched" almonds for a slightly higher price than unskinned almonds.

1   Put the nuts through a nut grinder or grind them in a food processor. If you haven't got either of these tools, put the nuts in a double plastic bag and pound them with a rolling pin. You are trying to break up the nuts into the smallest possible pieces.

2 After the nuts are ground, put them into a fresh plastic bag and roll the rolling pin on them with as much pressure as possible. (Hydraulic presses are used commercially to extract oil from olives and peanuts.) The nut particles will begin to cling together as the oil is pressed from the nut meat. The finer the nut meat, the better the butter will be.

3 When the butter is as finely pressed as you can get it, use a spatula to scrape it into a jar. Store the nut butter, covered, in the refrigerator, as it spoils easily.

4 Nut butters can be used as spreads on bread and crackers. Try a nut butter and jelly sandwich for a variation on an old favorite (use it with your homemade grape jelly from page 65).

BUTTER

COALESCING FAT DROPLETS FROM A SUSPENSION

Milk has often been called the most complete food. It contains water, carbohydrates, vitamins, minerals, proteins, and fat. Butter is made by extracting the fat from the other parts of milk. Cream contains more butterfat than whole milk. Use it to make butter in the next experiment.

MATERIALS & EQUIPMENT

- ½ pint heavy cream
- a pint jar with a tight cover
- a clean marble
- friends (optional, but there is a lot of shaking needed)

PROCEDURE

1 Put the cream in the jar with the marble. Screw on the cover and make sure that there are no leaks.

2 Shake the jar in a figure-eight motion. Note: This is a very strenuous activity. Be prepared to shake vigorously for 10 minutes. At first you will hear the marble moving. After a while, the cream will become so thick that you won't be able to feel the marble moving. Then, suddenly, the butter will form.

3 Drain the buttermilk—which is also good to drink—from the butter. Wash the butter by running cold tap water into the jar to remove any trapped buttermilk. Fish out the marble and pack the butter down. Store in the refrigerator. It will keep for two or three days.

OBSERVATIONS

The process of making butter takes advantage of certain properties of fat. When milk first comes from a cow, the butterfat is in the form of droplets that are suspended in the liquid. If fresh, whole milk is allowed to stand, the fat droplets rise to the top, carrying along some liquid. This is cream, and it is less dense than the more watery part of the milk, which is why it rises.

Cream is a fat-in-water emulsion. The fat droplets are held in suspension by milk proteins. The butter-making process is the formation of a water-in-fat emulsion where watery droplets are suspended in the fat.

When you make butter from cream, you force the fat droplets to come together by shaking the container. The droplets form larger and larger globules until they separate from the watery part of the mixture. This process is called *coalescing*. Butterfat coalesces because the fat globules are more attracted to one another than they are to the water in which they are suspended. The marble stirs up the mixture as you shake it, increasing the opportunity of fat droplets from different parts of the mixture to come in contact with one another.

The amount of butterfat varies in cream. Light cream has much less butterfat than heavy cream. The amount of fat in cream is the most important factor in making good whipped cream. Try making whipped cream from heavy cream and light cream. Which whips more easily? Which keeps its stiffness longer? If you whip cream too long, guess what happens? Butter!

AN ICE CREAM TASTE TEST

You may consider yourself an expert on ice cream, but do you really know a good ice cream when you taste it? Is there a real measurable difference between expensive premium brands and less expensive ice creams? How can you measure something that depends on personal opinion? The next experiment is designed to eliminate the variables that shape opinion. You will need a group of people to sample different ice creams and evaluate them. The larger the group the better, but even a group of five or six friends can give you some idea of which ice cream is the favorite.

MATERIALS & EQUIPMENT

For each person taking the test:

- a spoon

- a glass of water

- a napkin

- pen and paper

- an Ice Cream Taste Test Data Sheet copied from this book (see page 76)

- 4 plastic bowls of four different colors

4 different kinds of vanilla ice cream:

- 1 moderately priced brand that is also labeled "premium"

- 1 premium brand (The word "premium" must appear on the package. Usually it is more expensive and sold in pint containers.)

- 1 ice milk or vanilla frozen yogurt

- 1 very inexpensive brand

PROCEDURE

If you are conducting this experiment, you cannot participate in the test. Here's the setup:

1 Put a different ice cream in each bowl and make a record of the color and the kind of ice cream. Don't throw out the containers the ice cream came in. Also make a note of the prices paid for each brand.

2 Don't let the participants see the containers. They should see only the ice cream in the bowls at the time of the experiment. Packaging and brand names can have a large effect on how people "taste" ice cream. Don't tell them anything about the ice cream they will taste, only that they will be sampling four vanilla ice creams.

3 Some of the other things that could influence how people perceive the different ice cream tastes are conversation between participants, the

ICE CREAM TASTE TEST DATA SHEET

FILL IN THE BLANKS WITH A "YES" OR A "NO"

BOWL	#1	#2	#3	#4
FLAVOR				
Too much vanilla				
Too little vanilla				
Too sweet				
Not sweet enough				
Too sour				
Too salty				
Cooked				
Aftertaste				
BODY AND TEXTURE				
Coarse/icy				
Crumbly				
Fluffy				
Gummy				
Grainy				
APPEARANCE				
Color Too yellow				
Too white				
Melting Frothy melt				
Mouthfeel Creamy				
Smooth				
Chewy				
TOTAL NUMBER OF "NO" VOTES				

order in which they taste the ice cream, and leftover flavor from the last ice cream tasted. So you must instruct your participants not to speak to or look at one another. They should take a sip of water between tastes and sample each ice cream at least three or four times, in different orders, before drawing any conclusions.

4 Here are some of the things professional ice cream taste testers look for. Share this list with your participants:

COLOR—The color should be what you expect for the flavor. Vanilla is not too yellow or too white.

MELTING—The best ice cream melts quickly at room temperature, and the melted ice cream is a smooth liquid without foamy bubbles.

BODY AND TEXTURE—The best ice cream is firm but drips easily. The "mouthfeel" is creamy, smooth, and chewy. Better ice creams have more butterfat and stay firm at a higher temperature. They don't feel as cold as less expensive ice creams that have such a cold feel they can give you a headache.

FLAVOR—Vanilla ice cream should be pleasantly sweet and you should be able to taste the vanilla. The ice cream should not taste "cooked" like milk that has been boiled.

5 The tasters should fill out the data sheet with a "yes" or a "no" comparing the four different bowls of ice cream. After they have finished collecting their own data, add up the total number of "no" votes for each ice cream for the group. The ice cream with the most "no" votes wins.

OBSERVATIONS

Which ice cream wins? Do people generally prefer the most expensive ice cream?

Look at the list of ingredients on the cartons. All ice cream contains butterfat (in cream), milk, sugar, flavoring, and air that has been beaten in. Premium ice creams have more fat and less air than cheaper ice creams. High fat content lets the ice cream remain firm at warmer temperatures (like butter, which stays solid at room temperature). Premium ice creams melt without leaving behind a foam. Cheap ice creams have less fat and more air. Ice crystals tend to be larger and the ice cream feels colder. Emulsifiers and stabilizers are added to keep the size of the ice crystals small, but they can give the product a sticky, gummy texture and a strange aftertaste. The temperature, texture, and mouthfeel can tell you a lot about the ingredients. In general, premium ice creams have fewer ingredients than cheaper ice creams.

This kind of testing is done with huge numbers of participants by food manufacturers. It is no accident that they arrive at a formula for an ice cream that will appeal to the greatest number of people. The additives they put in cheaper ice creams allow for a longer shelf life in a freezer at a lower price point.

With practice you can become a champion ice cream tester.

NOTES

PROTEINS

In the eighteenth century, scientists became interested in a substance, found in all living things, that acted differently from all other substances. When a fluid like blood or egg white was heated, it did not become a boiling liquid like water or oil. Instead, it became a solid. And, as if this was not strange enough, once changed to a solid, it could never again be a liquid. Nothing could be done to return blood or egg white to its original liquid state. It did not take scientists long to realize that this strange material that changed permanently when heated was the very basis of all life. For this reason, they named it *protein*, meaning "of first importance."

Proteins have turned out to be the most complicated and diverse of all the compounds found in living things. Some proteins, like egg white, dissolve in water; some, like hair, are fibers. Some, like muscle protein, are responsible for movement in animals. But all proteins have certain things in common. In addition to the elements carbon, hydrogen, and oxygen, all proteins contain nitrogen. The atoms of these elements, along with an occasional atom of sulfur, form small molecules called *amino acids*. Proteins are chains of amino acids.

Only twenty different amino acids make up most proteins. The different amino acids are like an alphabet for proteins. When you think of all you can say with twenty-six letters, you can see how twenty amino acids can be used to form so many different kinds of proteins. A protein molecule can be thought of as a chemical sentence or even a paragraph. And the proteins of each kind of organism make up the unique language of that organism.

When human beings and other animals digest food, they are breaking down the protein they have eaten into amino acids. The amino acids from food are reassembled to build new proteins that are the particular type for that organism. So while sugars, starches, and fats are needed for energy, proteins are needed to build all the molecules that allow you to grow and repair the tissues of your body as you live your life. Most of the cells in the body of an adult are less than ten years old. You need to eat protein to constantly renew yourself.

Scientists have found protein to be one of the most challenging kinds of material to study. You can use some of their methods of investigation to learn how different kinds of protein behave and how some of the properties of certain proteins are important in food preparation.

MERINGUES
THE PROPERTIES OF EGG WHITES

An egg white is a good place to start learning about proteins. It is made up of about 87 percent water, about 9 percent protein, and a trace of minerals. The protein in an egg white makes it very useful for preparing food with different textures and consistencies.

MATERIALS & EQUIPMENT

- 3 eggs

- water

- a knife

- a deep bowl

- a plastic ice cube tray

- plastic wrap

- 2 small transparent glasses

- a flashlight

- a spoon

- an electric mixer or eggbeater

- a magnifying glass

PROCEDURE

1   Let the eggs come to room temperature. Protein in egg white is most useful to cooks at about 79°F (26°C). (You can check this out by trying to make meringues from egg whites at different temperatures.)

2   Separate the whites from the yolks using the instructions on pages 238–239, putting the whites into a deep bowl. Save the yolks; you'll need them for a later experiment. Put each egg yolk in its own compartment of a plastic ice cube tray, leaving empty compartments between the yolks. Cover the tray with plastic wrap and refrigerate.

3   Put enough egg whites into a glass to make a depth of 2 inches. Shine a beam of light through the egg white. Can you see the beam from the side as it passes through? The beam is an example of the Tyndall effect. (See chapter 3, page 36, if you don't remember the Tyndall effect.) What does it tell you about the size of the particles in egg white? It has been proven that protein particles are single molecules. They are among the largest molecules in existence.

4   Pour the egg whites back into the bowl. Put some water in the glass. Take about a teaspoon of egg white and stir it into the water. Does the egg white dissolve?

5   Beat the egg whites in the bowl with an electric mixer or eggbeater until they are foamy but will still flow if poured. Take about ½ teaspoon of foam and put it in a fresh glass of water. Does it dissolve? What shape are the tiny particles that are suspended in the water? Use a magnifying glass to check.

OBSERVATIONS

You have just demonstrated a very important property of proteins—that is, that the shape of a protein molecule plays an important part in determining how it behaves. Protein molecules in egg whites are like tiny balls of yarn. Their round, compact shape enables them to dissolve in water. When you beat egg whites, you are, in effect, unraveling these balls of yarn. The long chains that are pulled out are too large to dissolve. The process of changing protein from its natural form is call *denaturing*. It is impossible to restore denatured egg white to its original form.

Beating eggs is one form of denaturation. You can see other kinds of denaturation if you use them to make meringues, which show some other properties of proteins.

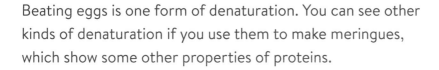

MATERIALS & EQUIPMENT

- oil

- ½ teaspoon cream of tartar

- ½ teaspoon salt

- ½ teaspoon vanilla extract

- 1 cup superfine sugar

- 3 egg whites, beaten foamy in previous experiment

- a cookie sheet

Continued . . .

- brown paper from a brown paper bag

- measuring cups and spoons

- an electric mixer or eggbeater

- an airtight container

- a rubber spatula

PROCEDURE

1 Preheat the oven to 175°F (79°C). Prepare a cookie sheet by covering it with brown paper rubbed with a little oil to coat.

2 Add the cream of tartar, salt, and vanilla extract to your bowl of foamy egg whites. Cream of tartar is an acid that makes the foam last longer. (You can test this idea with a simple side experiment: Beat 2 egg whites in separate bowls. Add ⅓ teaspoon cream of tartar to 1 egg white before you beat it. Find out which foam lasts longer.)

3 Beat the egg whites with an electric mixer or eggbeater until you can make peaks that stand upright. As the egg whites are beaten, the protein becomes more and more unraveled, and the foam becomes stiffer and stiffer.

4 Slowly add the sugar by sprinkling a tablespoon at a time over the egg whites. Continue beating while adding the sugar. Occasionally scrape down the sides of the bowl with a rubber spatula.

5 The water in the egg whites is carried along the strands of protein. When the sugar is beaten into stiff egg whites, it dissolves into this water. This is why you use superfine sugar (which dissolves more easily), and you add it

very slowly to give it a chance to go into solution. If all the sugar doesn't dissolve, tiny droplets of sugar syrup will form on the surface of the finished product. Professional chefs consider such a "weeping" meringue a failure.

6 After you have added all the sugar, taste the meringue. It should not feel gritty, but if it does, beat in a tablespoon of water to dissolve all the sugar.

7 Make four separate piles of meringue on the oiled paper. Push down the middle of each pile to make a bowl shape.

8 The last step in making a meringue is to remove the water. This is accomplished by drying it in a warm oven for a long time.

9 Put the meringues in the oven for 1 hour. At the end of that time, turn off the oven and let the meringues stay in the oven overnight.

10 A successful meringue is a stiff, snow-white confection that will keep for weeks in an airtight container. (Since sugar absorbs moisture from the air, meringues must be stored away from the air. Otherwise, they become soft and fall apart.)

11 Fill the meringues with fruit or ice cream and top with whipped cream or chocolate sauce. Yum!

HOW TO SAVE EGG YOLKS

Egg yolks contain the nutrients needed to nourish a growing chick. Since they can also provide nourishment for countless bacteria, they are among the most perishable of leftovers. One way to preserve food is to freeze it. Water in frozen food is solid ice and is not available to microorganisms. That's why freezing can preserve food. But freezing can also make the yolk unusable unless you are an inventive chef. Do the next experiment to see if there is a way around this problem.

MATERIALS & EQUIPMENT

- 3 egg yolks
- ⅛ teaspoon salt
- ⅛ teaspoon sugar
- a plastic ice cube tray
- measuring spoons
- a spoon
- paper
- a pencil
- plastic wrap
- a knife

PROCEDURE

1 Take the egg yolks you saved from the last experiment out of the refrigerator. Put the salt in one egg yolk and stir it well with a spoon. Rinse off the spoon. Put the sugar in another egg yolk and stir. Rinse the spoon again and stir the third egg yolk, but don't put anything in it.

2 Draw a diagram of the ice cube tray showing where each egg yolk is located. Cover the tray with plastic wrap and put it in the freezer overnight.

3 The next day, let the yolks defrost at room temperature. Stick a knife into each one (rinsing off between dips). See whether the egg yolk is a firm semisolid or still runny. You can use the runny egg yolks to make cupcakes. The semisolid yolk is perfectly edible, but not too tasty.

OBSERVATIONS

The egg yolk is about half water. The solids are mostly fats and some proteins. Some of the proteins are dissolved in the water phase of the egg yolk. But most of the yolk proteins and all the fat are in tiny round particles that are suspended in the liquid creating a thick emulsion. When you hard-boil an egg, the soft, crumbly, grainy texture of the yolk is due to the denaturing of the granular proteins.

When an egg yolk is frozen, the protein in the water solution is denatured, trapping the water and producing a solid mass when it is defrosted. If you add salt or sugar to an egg yolk, however, some of the water is removed from its close connection with protein. It is not trapped in the denatured protein after defrosting, so the egg yolks remain runny.

A QUICK CUPCAKE RECIPE

MATERIALS & EQUIPMENT

- ½ stick (¼ cup) butter, softened

- ½ cup sugar

- 2 egg yolks

- ⅓ cup milk

- 1 cup cake flour (not self-rising)

- 1⅓ teaspoons baking powder

- ¼ teaspoon salt

- ¾ teaspoon vanilla extract

- measuring cups and spoons

- 2 medium bowls

- a sifter

- a cupcake/muffin pan

- cupcake liners

- an electric mixer or fork

PROCEDURE

1   Preheat the oven to 350°F (177°C). Beat the softened butter in a bowl with the sugar. Then beat in the egg yolks.

2   In another bowl, sift together the cake flour, baking powder, and salt.

3   Pour the milk and vanilla into a measuring cup. Add about one-third of the dry ingredients to the butter-sugar mixture. Then beat in half the milk mixture, then another third of the dry ingredients, then the rest of the milk, and then the last of the dry ingredients. You should beat the batter well after each addition.

4   Line 4 wells of the cupcake/muffin pan with cupcake liners, pour the batter into them, and bake for 25 to 30 minutes.

CUSTARD

COAGULATING PROTEIN

The process of changing liquid protein into a solid by heating it is called *coagulation*. Coagulation is a kind of denaturing. You used coagulated egg white to clarify stock in chapter 3 (see pages 48–51). Egg white coagulates at about 156°F (69°C). It changes from an almost colorless, transparent, fairly thick liquid to a white solid. The protein in an egg yolk also coagulates when heated.

Protein coagulation is one of the main reasons the texture of food changes when it is cooked. Meat and fish become firm, and batters change from liquids to solids. In fact, most baked goods have a "skeleton" of coagulated milk or egg protein that supports them.

Custard is a homogeneous mixture of eggs, milk, and sugar that has been heated to coagulate the protein in the eggs and the milk. The next experiment shows how different amounts of heat affect the coagulation of these proteins.

MATERIALS & EQUIPMENT

- ½ cup sugar
- ⅛ teaspoon salt
- 1 teaspoon vanilla extract
- 2 cups milk
- 3 eggs
- measuring cups and spoon

- a bowl
- an electric mixer or eggbeater
- 4 custard cups or other ovenproof cups
- a roasting pan the cups will fit into
- water

PROCEDURE

1   Preheat the oven to 325°F (163°C). Beat the sugar, salt, and vanilla into the milk. Add the eggs and beat well.

2   Divide the mixture equally among the custard cups. Set the cups in the roasting pan and pour about an inch of water into the pan. (This is to make sure that the bottoms of the cups are not heated more than any other part.) Put the pan with the custards in the oven.

3   After 30 minutes, remove one cup of custard. Take the second cup out after 40 minutes, the third cup after 50 minutes, and the fourth cup after 1 hour.

OBSERVATIONS

Which custard has been properly cooked? Which custard has separated and has the most liquid?

When eggs first coagulate, the protein is able to trap and hold other liquids, such as the water in the milk and egg whites. If eggs are cooked too long or at too high a temperature, they become tougher and tougher and can no longer hold water. For example, scrambled eggs from which water has separated have been either overcooked or cooked too quickly.

Properly made custard is a smooth, shiny, yellow pudding that slices cleanly when you put a spoon into it. There is no trace of water from either the egg or the milk.

All these custards are good to eat. Refrigerate them until you are ready to serve them. The overcooked custards should be drained before eating. They can be topped with fruit.

SOUR MILK BISCUITS

PROTEIN DENATURED BY ACID

Some protein is easily denatured by acid. You can tell when this happens if solid particles form in a liquid that contains dissolved protein, like milk. The protein in sour milk makes the milk thicker and ultimately separates from the water portion of the milk. Certain bacteria make milk sour. Their acid waste products denature milk protein. But you can make a quick version of sour milk by adding your own acid.

Bring ½ cup of milk to room temperature. Put 2 teaspoons of vinegar, a weak acid, in another cup. Pour the milk into the vinegar and stir. Let the mixture stand for about 10 minutes. How can you tell if the protein is denatured? Stir the milk. Can you get the denatured protein to dissolve?

You can use the sour milk to make biscuits. Just substitute it for whole milk in a package of biscuit mix and follow the directions on the box, or make your own biscuits from scratch using this recipe.

MATERIALS & EQUIPMENT

- 1 cup flour

- 1 teaspoon
  baking powder

- ⅛ teaspoon
  baking soda

- ½ teaspoon salt

- 2 tablespoons
  cold butter

- ½ cup sour milk

- a medium bowl

- a pastry blender
  or 2 knives

- a fork

- a spoon

- a cookie sheet

PROCEDURE

1   Preheat the oven to 450°F (232°C). In a medium bowl, mix together the flour, baking powder, baking soda, and salt.

2   Using a pastry blender or two knives, cut in the butter (see instructions pages 236–237) until the mixture looks like crumbs the size of small peas.

3   Add the sour milk and stir with a fork until all the ingredients are thoroughly combined.

4   Drop by spoonfuls onto the ungreased cookie sheet. Bake for 12 to 15 minutes, until golden brown.

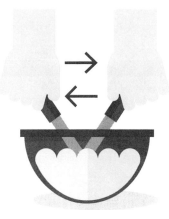

GELATIN
SOL-GEL TRANSFORMATION

If all protein were as easily denatured as the soluble proteins in egg and milk, life could not survive. About 40 percent of the protein in our bodies and those of other animals is considerably tougher than egg and milk protein. It already exists as a solid that will not dissolve in water. This protein, called *collagen*, is found in cartilage, the white flexible material at the ends of bones. It is also found in tendons, which attach muscles to bones, and ligaments, which tie bones together; and it is the main protein in bones themselves. Collagen is the protein that keeps us from falling apart.

As you might expect, collagen is also found in meat we eat. Tougher cuts of meat contain more collagen than more tender cuts. The problem facing cooks is how to make the collagen softer and the meat more tender.

Fortunately, this is not a difficult task. When collagen is heated with water for a while, it breaks down into a smaller, softer, soluble protein called *gelatin*. The process of changing collagen to gelatin is speeded up with the addition of an acid like lemon juice, vinegar, or tomatoes to the cooking water. (Some cooks soak or marinate tough meats in vinegar before stewing.) A tomato stew should become tender sooner than one made in meat broth alone. Can you design an experiment to confirm this?

If you would like to prepare almost pure gelatin, get two or three veal bones from your butcher. Veal bones, which come from young calves, have a great deal of cartilage. (As animals grow older, cartilage is replaced with bone.) Cover the veal bones with water and boil for an hour. Strain the broth and let it cool. You can improve the taste of the gelatin in the broth by adding tomato juice. See what happens to the broth when you refrigerate it.

Gelatin is different from collagen. Gelatin dissolves in hot water, while collagen doesn't dissolve at all. You can learn about some other properties of gelatin in the next experiment.

MATERIALS & EQUIPMENT

- ½ cup cold water
- a package of unflavored gelatin
- 1½ cups boiling water
- a package of presweetened Kool-Aid
- a measuring cup
- a small bowl
- a wooden spoon
- a clear glass
- a flashlight
- a small pot
- a 2-cup mold or 2-cup container
- a plate

PROCEDURE

1   Pour the cold water into a bowl and sprinkle the package of gelatin over it. Does the gelatin attract the water? How can you tell?

2   When the gelatin has been softened, add the boiling water and stir. Does

the gelatin dissolve? This mixture is called a *sol*.

3 Pour some of the sol into a clear glass. Shine a light through it. Does it show the Tyndall effect (see page 36)? What does this tell you about the size of gelatin molecules?

4 Let the sol cool in the glass, and then chill it, uncovered. The most dramatic property of gelatin is revealed when a sol cools. It changes from a liquid to a semisolid quivering mass called a *gel*. Shine a light through the gel. Does it show the same Tyndall effect as the sol? Is there any sign of water in the gel?

5 Put the gel in a pot and warm it over medium heat. Can you change the gel back into a sol by adding heat? Add ½ package of presweetened Kool-Aid to the sol and stir with a wooden spoon until it is dissolved. Pour the flavored gelatin mixture into a mold, let cool, and then chill until set.

6 You can remove the set gelatin from the mold by changing the gel next to the mold back into a sol. Fill the sink with hot water and have ready a plate large enough to cover the top of the mold. Put the mold into the water for about 10 seconds. Be careful not to let any water get on the gelatin. After

removing the mold from the sink, put the plate over it, turn the whole thing over, and give it a hard shake. You should hear the gelatin plop onto the plate. If the gelatin doesn't slip out, put the mold in the hot water again for a few seconds and repeat the procedure. Be careful that you don't heat it too much, as you can lose the sharp shape of the mold on your dessert.

7   A gelatin dessert can be unmolded long before it is to be served. Just return it to the refrigerator until you are ready to eat it.

OBSERVATIONS

The sol-gel transformation fascinated scientists. They wondered what happened to the water. Their research discovered that the water is trapped by a network of gelatin molecules that form when gelatin cools. They also discovered that as gelatin ages, it is able to hold less and less water.

See for yourself how gelatin loses moisture as it ages. Cut some of your gelatin dessert into 1-inch cubes. Leave the cubes, uncovered, on a plate in the refrigerator for several days. Every morning and evening, eat a cube to see how they begin to get tougher and tougher as they age.

Human skin, which is largely collagen, also loses its ability to hold moisture as it ages. Many beauty face creams advertise that they add collagen to skin. I'm curious how they do that, since collagen is an insoluble protein. Beware scientific jargon in advertising.

MUFFINS

A STUDY OF GLUTEN— THE WHEAT PROTEIN

Denatured protein is the "skeleton" that supports baked products. In cakes and muffins and other delicate baked goods, this support comes from coagulated milk and eggs. In bread, the support comes from a protein called *gluten* found in wheat flour.

Flour does not actually contain gluten. It contains two substances that can become gluten under the right conditions. The next experiment will show you some of the conditions needed to develop gluten and the effect of different amounts of gluten on the texture of muffins.

MATERIALS & EQUIPMENT

- 1 cup all-purpose flour
- 2 tablespoons sugar
- 1 teaspoon salt
- 2 teaspoons baking powder
- 2 tablespoons butter
- 2 eggs
- 1 cup cake flour (not self-rising)
- ⅔ cup milk

- paper muffin-cup liners
- a 12-cup muffin tin
- 2 spoons
- measuring cups and spoons
- waxed paper
- a sifter
- an electric mixer or eggbeater
- a small frying pan
- 3 bowls

PROCEDURE

1   Preheat the oven to 350°F (177°C). Put eight muffin-cup liners in the muffin tin, four in each side so you make two groups separated by four empty cups in the center. Use different-colored liners on each side or double line one side to help keep track of which cups hold which batter.

2   Sift about 1 cup of all-purpose flour onto a sheet of waxed paper. All-purpose flour contains more protein that can become gluten than cake flour. Measure out 1 cup of this flour and resift it together with 1 tablespoon of the sugar, ½ teaspoon of the salt, and 1 teaspoon of the baking powder into a bowl.

3   Using a clean piece of waxed paper, repeat this process with cake flour instead of all-purpose flour. Cake flour has a lower potential gluten content. This mixture will be prepared in a way that keeps the gluten from developing.

4   Melt 1 tablespoon of the butter in a frying pan and let it cool. In a clean bowl, beat ⅓ cup of the milk with 1 egg. Add the cooled, melted butter and pour the mixture into the dry ingredients containing the all-purpose flour. Mix carefully until all the flour is moist, then beat the batter until it becomes smooth and glossy.

5 Repeat the steps for melting butter and mixing it with milk and egg. Add this second mixture all at once to the bowl with the cake flour. Stir quickly and lightly until all the flour is moist. You should not have to stir for more than 15 seconds. Do not beat too hard, and don't worry about lumps in the batter. How does this batter look compared with the other batter?

6 Spoon the batter containing the cake flour into four of the muffin cups. Then spoon the all-purpose flour batter into the other four cups. Bake for 15 minutes, until the tops are brown. Let the muffins cool.

OBSERVATIONS

Cut one of each kind of muffin in half. Which muffin has the finer grain? Which makes crumbs more easily? Taste the muffins. Which is more tender? Which has large tunnels caused by larger bubbles of gas?

Gluten develops when dough is warm and there is a lot of mixing. Gluten is prevented from developing when dough is kept cold and handled as little as possible. Some bread does not contain any protein other than gluten. Why do you think bread dough is kneaded? Why should pie dough be handled lightly and as little as possible?

There are many variations of this experiment. Try making muffins with cake flour and with bread flour. Handle the batters the same way. See if temperature affects the way gluten develops. Use all-purpose flour but use ice-cold ingredients in one batter and room-temperature ingredients in the other. Which of the following baked products do you think depend on gluten for structure and which must be fairly gluten-free to remain flaky and tender: bread, cream puffs, pie crust, cake, biscuits? Can you think up experiments to test your ideas?

notes

KITCHEN CHEMISTRY

The first chemists, called *alchemists*, were not searching for truth about nature or looking for a system to describe all matter. They worked long, hard hours over smelly cauldrons, which often contained dangerous materials, with a single idea to keep them going—finding a way to create gold. Nothing noble here. Just another get-rich-quick scheme.

You can't blame an alchemist for trying. Suppose you had plunged an iron pot into a perfectly ordinary-looking spring and found upon removing the pot some time later that it was covered with a red coating. You might reason, as they did, that if you could turn iron into something else, why not look for a way to make gold from other metals? To this end, alchemists separated mixtures and mixed substances together. They developed many procedures used in laboratories today, and they discovered many substances no one knew existed.

But the alchemists failed in their intended purpose. No matter how hard they tried, they could not make gold. They only produced gold if they started with it. The alchemists didn't know that no one can make gold, for gold is an element—a substance that cannot be broken down. But alchemists did make many other important discoveries. Perhaps the most important were the events they observed in which one kind of matter did change into another. These events are *chemical reactions*.

There are countless numbers of different chemical reactions. The flame from a gas burner, the rust on an old piece of iron, and the browning of a cut apple are three examples. Despite the obvious differences, all chemical reactions have certain things in common.

In every chemical reaction, you start with one kind of matter and end up with another. Often the products of a reaction have very different properties from the reactants you began with. For example, when propane gas in a stove reacts with oxygen in the air, the products are carbon dioxide and water vapor. This reaction can be written as a chemical equation:

propane gas + oxygen + starter heat → carbon dioxide + water + flame

All chemical reactions involve energy, which may be in the form of heat, light, or electricity. Chemists usually find heat is the easiest way to measure energy involved in reactions. All chemical reactions can be divided into one of two kinds: those that give off heat and those that take up heat. Some reactions, like burning, need a small amount of heat to get started but give off energy once they get going.

Many times a chemical reaction is not as apparent as the flame of a gas burner. There are other ways of knowing when a chemical reaction has taken place. In this chapter, you will learn some of these ways, and how chemical reactions play a significant part in the preparation of food.

LEMON FIZZ

A REACTION FORMS A GAS

Sometimes a gas is the product of a chemical reaction. If the reaction takes place in a solution, bubbles rise to the surface and are easy to see.

MATERIALS & EQUIPMENT

- water
- 1 teaspoon baking soda
- lemonade
- measuring spoons
- 2 glass tumblers
- 2 spoons

PROCEDURE

1 Fill one glass half full of water. Add ½ teaspoon of the baking soda and stir with one of your spoons. Does the baking soda dissolve easily? Is there any reaction? Use red cabbage indicator (see chapter 2, pages 20–22) to test this solution to see if it is an acid or a base. Pour a little of the solution into a small amount of the indicator.

2   Fill a second glass half full of lemonade. Test the lemonade with the indicator in another container. Using a clean spoon, stir the remaining baking soda into the lemonade. How can you tell that there was a reaction? Drink the lemon fizz quickly before all the bubbles escape into the air.

OBSERVATIONS

Invent other experiments to see if baking soda reacts with other acid drinks. Try making orange fizz or apple fizz.

Baking soda is a compound of sodium, carbon, hydrogen, and oxygen. It reacts with acids to give off carbon dioxide.

CUPCAKES
HOW CAKES RISE

The changes that occur as a cake bakes are very dramatic. As the batter gets warmer, tiny bubbles of gas form in the mixture and grow larger. The batter surrounding these bubbles becomes permanently set as the protein from milk and eggs coagulates with heat. Flour strengthens the walls of these bubbles so the cake doesn't collapse when removed from the oven. Sugar and flour hold moisture to make the cake tender. The ingredients play an important part in the structure of a cake. Perhaps the most remarkable thing about this amazing structure is that it is delicious to eat.

Since the source of the lightness and delicacy of a cake is gas bubbles, it's fun to investigate the bubble-producing reactions. Then we'll investigate how bubbles help make a cake rise.

MATERIALS & EQUIPMENT

- ½ teaspoon cream of tartar

- water

- ½ teaspoon baking soda

- teaspoon double-acting baking powder, divided in 2

- measuring spoons

- 4 glass tumblers

- 4 spoons

- a small saucepan

- a candy thermometer

PROCEDURE 1

1 Put the cream of tartar in half a glass of cold water. Stir to dissolve. Is there any reaction? Test a small amount of the solution with red cabbage indicator (see chapter 2, pages 20–22). Is it an acid or a base?

2 Add the baking soda to the cream of tartar solution. Be sure to wipe off your measuring spoon before you dip it into the baking soda box and use a clean spoon to stir the mixture.

OBSERVATIONS

Is there any reaction? What gas is released? How would your findings from Lemon Fizz predict this result?

There used to be a baking powder product made with cream of tartar (also known as tartaric acid), baking soda, and cornstarch. Cream of tartar is an acid that can be packaged in a dry form and dissolves quickly in liquid. The cornstarch absorbs moisture in the powder mixture so that the baking soda and cream of tartar are prevented from reacting with each other in the box. Batter made with cream of tartar baking powder had to be baked as soon as it was mixed. If it stood around for a while before baking, most of the gas (created from the acid interacting with the oxygen and carbon in the baking soda) escaped, and the cake did not rise as much. You can test this idea with the cupcake recipe and some experimental procedures given in the next section.

PROCEDURE 2

1 Half fill one glass with cold water and a second glass with hot water. Add ½ teaspoon of the double-acting baking powder to each glass. In which glass is the reaction stronger?

2 When no more bubbles are coming out in the first glass, heat the solution in a pan. Is there a second reaction?

OBSERVATIONS

A second type of baking powder was developed that could stand around and wait in batter before being baked. It contained an acid called sodium aluminum sulfate, which reacted with baking soda only when heated. So the carbon dioxide would be produced only when the cake was being baked.

There were two problems with baking powder containing sodium aluminum sulfate. First, it left a bitter aftertaste in the cake. Second, for certain recipes, the heat of the oven might set the structure of the cake before any gas was released, forming a very heavy product. For this reason, double-acting baking powder was developed. It contains two acid powders: a quick-acting acid powder, like cream of tartar, that starts releasing carbon dioxide as soon as it is mixed with liquid, and sodium aluminum sulfate, to release more carbon dioxide when it is baked. Less of this acid is needed in such a powder, so there is less bitter aftertaste.

PROCEDURE 3

1 Heat water until it is about 150°F (66°C). (Use a candy thermometer to measure temperature.) Half fill a glass tumbler with the hot water. Put the candy thermometer in the water.

2 When the temperature reading levels off and stays the same for about 5 seconds, add the remaining heaping teaspoon of double-acting baking powder and stir.

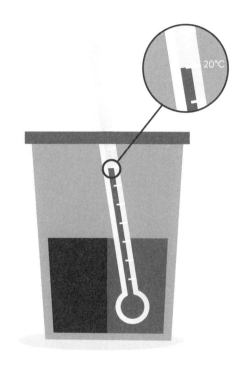

OBSERVATIONS

Watch the thermometer as the reaction takes place. Does the solution get warmer or colder? By how many degrees? You can repeat this experiment using different amounts of baking powder.

What you have just witnessed is an example of a chemical reaction that takes up heat. Unlike combustion, in which heat is given off, the chemical reaction in which sodium aluminum sulfate breaks down and releases carbon dioxide requires heat to begin. The heat for this reaction is removed from the surrounding liquid, making it cooler.

Use the cupcake recipe on the next page in the following experiments, which reveal how different baking powders act in batter.

BASIC CUPCAKE RECIPE

MATERIALS & EQUIPMENT

- 1 cup cake flour (not self-rising)
- ½ cup sugar
- ¼ teaspoon salt
- 1 egg
- ½ stick (¼ cup) butter
- ¼ cup milk

- 1 teaspoon double-acting baking powder
- 1 teaspoon vanilla extract
- 2 bowls
- waxed paper
- measuring cups and spoons

- a sifter
- an electric mixer
- a spoon
- 12-cup muffin tin
- paper muffin-tin liners (optional)

BASIC PROCEDURE

1   Preheat the oven to 350°F (177°C). Sift the flour onto waxed paper and then measure. Resift the flour together with the sugar, salt, and baking

powder (or baking powder substitute, depending on the experiment) into a dry bowl. Set the dry ingredients aside.

2   In a separate bowl, beat the softened butter with an electric mixer. Next beat in the egg, milk, and vanilla.

3   Add the liquid ingredients to the dry ingredients all at once. Stir carefully until all the flour is moistened, then beat just until the batter is smooth.

4   Grease four wells of a muffin tin or line them with paper liners. Pour the batter into the prepared muffin cups. Bake for about 15 minutes. The cupcakes are done when the tops are brown and a toothpick stuck into a cupcake comes out clean.

VARIATION 1

Make two batches of cupcakes, substituting ½ teaspoon baking soda and ¼ teaspoon cream of tartar for the baking powder in each. Mix up the first batch and let it stand in its mixing bowl for at least an hour before you mix the second batch. Bake both batches at the same time.

VARIATION 2

Try making the cupcakes with different amounts of baking powder. Use ½ teaspoon for one batch, 1 teaspoon for a second batch, and 1½ teaspoons for a third batch.

VARIATION 3

If you want to try one large experiment, first mix a batter using ½ teaspoon cream of tartar and ¼ teaspoon baking soda instead of the baking powder. Let this batter stand for about a half hour and then mix two more batters. In the second batch, use the double-acting baking powder called for in the recipe. Then make a third batch the same as the first, using cream of tartar and baking soda. Bake all three batches together in a 12-cup muffin tin. Since each batch makes 4 cupcakes, you can use one muffin tin for the entire experiment.

When you compare cupcakes, look for differences in height, crumb size, and taste.

Note: It's fun to watch a cake bake. If you have an oven with a window, leave the light on and look in during the baking process. If you don't have such a window, don't open the oven before it is time for the cupcakes to be done. If a blast of cold air hits a cake before it is finished setting, the hot gas in the cake suddenly contracts and the cake falls. Since the center of a cake sets last, a draft often produces a cake with a fallen center.

CARAMEL SYRUP

SUGAR DECOMPOSES

Some compounds, like sugar, break down into simpler compounds and elements when heated. Sugar melts at 320°F (160°C) and starts to break down or decompose at 356°F (180°C). When sugar breaks down, water is one product and carbon is another. As more and more carbon forms, the liquid sugar becomes straw colored and eventually turns dark brown. Sugar that has been partly broken down is known as caramel.

You can see the chemical breakdown of sugar when you make caramel. Be very careful in following the directions for this experiment, because you will be working with very hot material. You should have an adult help you with this experiment.

MATERIALS & EQUIPMENT

- ½ cup sugar

- ½ cup water

- a small, heavy frying pan

- a wooden spoon

PROCEDURE

1 Put the sugar in a small, heavy frying pan. Stirring continuously, cook the sugar over medium heat. It will soon melt and start turning brown. When the sugar is straw colored, remove the pan from the heat.

2 *Slowly and carefully* add the water. The caramel will be brittle and very hot. If you add water too quickly, it may spatter and burn you.

VERY HOT STEAM ⟶

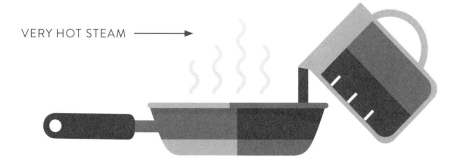

3 Return the pan to low heat and stir for about 10 minutes. Try to get all the caramel to dissolve. After 10 minutes, remove the pan from the heat and let the syrup cool.

OBSERVATIONS

When the syrup has cooled completely, taste it and compare the taste to sugar. Which is sweeter? You can serve this syrup over ice cream or use it to glaze the cupcakes from the last experiment.

For a second experiment, try heating ½ cup sugar until it is dark brown. Again, turn off the heat and add about ½ cup water. This time you will have to be even more careful, as the caramel is so hot there may be a violent reaction. A solution made of dark caramel is used to color gravies and stews. The sugar has been broken down so completely that no sweetness remains.

What change in the appearance of the sugar lets you know that a chemical reaction was taking place? Can you think of any other color changes that are the result of a chemical reaction?

ONIONS AND HAMBURGERS

THE MAILLARD REACTION AND CARAMELIZATION OF COOKING

The minute you walk in the door, you can tell that someone has been cooking onions and hamburgers. How? From the delicious aroma that fills the air. There are two important chemical reactions that take place in certain foods when they are exposed to high temperatures—or cooked. One is caramelization, which involves sugars reacting with other sugars to become brown and flavorful compounds when heated, as you saw in the last experiment. The other chemical reaction was discovered in 1912 by French biochemist Louis-Camille Maillard (*mah-YAR* is the French pronunciation). He discovered that dry heat of 310°F (154°C) will cause sugars to react with amino acids (from the proteins in the foods), as well as change color to brown. The *Maillard reaction* is responsible for causing the outsides of baked goods and meat to brown, and for the smell and darkening of roasted coffee beans. Not only does the heat cause a color change as the sugars are broken down, but it also produces many new molecules that enhance the flavor of the food.

Sautéed onions are a deep brown color and have a sweet taste due to caramelization. But the Maillard reaction also occurs with the amino acids present in the protein of the onion. If you've ever sautéed onions to the caramelized stage, you know that it takes patience. However, the process can be speeded up if you add an alkali or base. Do this experiment to see how.

MATERIALS & EQUIPMENT

- cooking spray
- about ½ cup chopped onions
- baking soda
- a ground-beef patty
- a nonstick frying pan
- 2 rubber spatulas
- a knife

PROCEDURE

1 Set the frying pan over medium heat. Spray the surface with cooking spray. Wait a minute or two for the pan to get hot. The spray will start to bubble.

2   Put the onions in the pan, dividing them into two groups with a space between them. Sprinkle one group with a pinch (a very small amount) of baking soda.

3   Sauté the two groups of onions, stirring them with a different spatula for each group. Remove the onions when they are browning at the edges, keeping the groups separated.

4   Wash the frying pan. Set it over medium heat and spray it again with cooking spray. Cut the hamburger patty in half. Sprinkle a tiny amount of baking soda on both sides of one half of the patty.

5   Fry the hamburger halves for about 2 minutes on one side, then turn them over and fry the other side. Notice the browning that takes place.

OBSERVATIONS

Which group of onions caramelized more quickly? Taste the onions. Which group tastes sweeter? Do a similar taste test with the hamburger. Which tastes sweeter? If you cook a hamburger in a microwave, there is no browning. That's because cooking in a microwave is all about heating water molecules, which change to a gas at 212°F (100°C). This is not hot enough for either reaction. You can eat hamburger that's been cooked in a microwave. You probably won't like it. You may also not like the taste of baking soda. So the Maillard reaction, without the taste of baking soda, takes patience to get right. No proper chef will hurry this process if he or she hopes to keep a job.

VITAMIN C FRUIT SALAD

OXIDATION OF FRUIT

Ever notice how certain fruits and vegetables turn brown when a cut surface is exposed to the air? This is a different kind of browning reaction than caramelization or Maillard. This happens because there is a pigment in fruit that reacts with the oxygen in air (more on this reaction in chapter 10). Oxygen is a very reactive element, which combines with many substances in a reaction called, fittingly, *oxidation*. Oxidation is a chemical reaction that always gives off energy. Combustion is oxidation of a fuel that is so rapid that a flame is produced. Rusting iron is slower oxidation that produces heat (but not so much that you'd notice it under ordinary conditions). When an apple turns brown, oxidation is also fairly slow.

Apples, peaches, pears, and bananas are all easily oxidized. A fresh fruit salad can be protected from oxidation, however, by keeping it from the air or by treating it with vitamin C. Do the next experiment and see how.

MATERIALS & EQUIPMENT

- water
- 1 chewable vitamin C tablet
- 1 apple
- 1 peach or pear
- 1 banana
- a small, deep bowl
- a sharp knife
- 2 shallow soup bowls
- a slotted spoon

PROCEDURE

1 Put about a cup of water in the small, deep bowl and dissolve the vitamin C tablet in it.

2 Cut the apple in half. Peel and cut out the core of one half quickly. Slice this half into the bowl of vitamin C solution. Make sure each slice is covered with the solution. Remove the apple slices with a slotted spoon and put them in one of the shallow bowls.

3 Peel, core, and then slice the other half of the apple directly into the other shallow bowl.

4 Repeat this procedure with the other fruits: Slice half into the vitamin C solution and leave the slices from the other half untreated. Put all the vitamin C pieces in one bowl and the untreated pieces in the other. Arrange the fruit so that as much surface is exposed to the air as possible.

5 Let the two fruit salads stand for an hour or more. Watch to see where browning occurs.

OBSERVATIONS

Can you see a difference between the treated and untreated fruit? Why do you think lemon juice is put on apple slices as they are being prepared for apple pie? Do lemons contain vitamin C? Other fruits and vegetables that brown when exposed to air are eggplants, avocados, and raw potatoes. Can you design an experiment to see if vitamin C slows down their oxidation?

Oxidation of fruit is affected by temperature. You can test this by making two fruit salads. Leave one at room temperature and put the other in the refrigerator. Which salad browns first?

The term *oxidation* is used by chemists for any reaction in which substances combine in a manner similar to the way they combine with oxygen. The oxidation reaction of these fruits is sped up because of a certain protein in the fruit known as an *enzyme* (more on enzymes in chapter 10). Before the fruit is cut, the enzyme and the compounds that will turn brown in the presence of oxygen are separated from each other. But when cells are injured as the fruit is cut, the enzyme and the compounds come in contact with each other and oxidation occurs. The enzyme is not present in melons and citrus fruits. They will eventually turn brown in air, but without the enzyme it takes days instead of minutes.

Fruits that oxidize easily will also react with copper and iron. Put a fruit salad in a copper bowl or an iron pan. Compare the browning of that salad with a fruit salad in a glass or china bowl. Cover these salads with plastic wrap to reduce oxidation with the air.

All the fruit salads in these experiments are good to eat, even if the fruit is discolored. Combine all the fruit when you have finished experimenting. Add a small can of apricots or some fruit syrup and chill before serving.

FRUIT AND TEA PUNCH
TESTING FOR IRON

For most people, a test tube symbolizes chemistry. The beauty of the test tube is that it allows the chemist to combine small amounts of material in a vessel where it is easy to see if a chemical reaction takes place.

There are several changes that let you know when a reaction is occurring. In the experiments you have done in this chapter up to now, you've seen reactions that produce a gas and reactions that produce a color change. Another indication that a reaction is taking place is if you see a clear solution become cloudy as solid particles form. Such solid particles are called *precipitates*. You will be looking for a precipitate in the next experiment.

If you have a chemistry set with test tubes, you can use them for this experiment—just be sure they have been cleaned thoroughly. If you don't, use small, clear, colorless juice glasses.

There are certain chemicals in tea that react with iron compounds in fruit juices to form a precipitate. This precipitate is very annoying if you are preparing a punch made with tea. All too often a crystal-clear iced tea punch becomes cloudy. Although the punch may taste fine, its muddy look is not what the party-giver had in mind. Not all fruits contain iron, however. Learn which ones do in the next experiment and keep your iced tea punch sparkling clear.

MATERIALS & EQUIPMENT

- 2 cups brewed strong black tea (room temperature)

- juice glasses or test tubes

- pen and paper

- an assortment of fruit juices, including canned and bottled juices, red juices, pineapple juice, and prune juice

PROCEDURE

1   Set out a row of small glasses or test tubes (in a rack to keep them vertical) and put about an inch of tea in each glass. Label the glasses for each juice you are going to test.

2   You might also want to prepare a data sheet to record your observations. Here is an example of what a data sheet might look like:

FRUIT JUICE	TEST RESULT
Orange	—
Canned pineapple	—
Cranberry	?
Cherry Hi-C	?

3   Add about an inch of juice to each glass or test tube of tea. Watch for cloudiness. If a precipitate forms, put a plus sign (+) next to the name of the juice on your data sheet. If no precipitate forms and the mixture remains clear, put a minus sign (−). If you are not certain, put a "?" on the data sheet and test the juice again. Some juices are cloudy to begin with. Make sure that a new precipitate forms by comparing the tea mixture with a plain sample of juice.

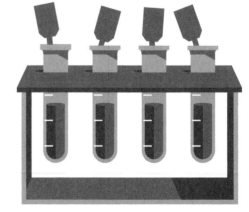

ORANGE   CANNED PINEAPPLE   CRANBERRY   CHERRY HI-C

OBSERVATIONS

Which juices contain iron? Do canned juices contain more iron than bottled juices? According to a table of food composition, which tells the various vitamins, minerals, fats, proteins, etc., in food, the juices that contain the most iron are red juices, pineapple juice, and prune juice. Do your findings agree with this?

When you have finished the experiment, pour all the mixtures into a pitcher. Taste it to see if you might like to add more of any particular juice. Add any leftover tea. Pour over ice to serve.

MANGO EGG YOLKS

MOLECULAR GASTRONOMY

There's a new kind of food preparation that employs some interesting principles of chemistry and physics. You can make spheres out of liquid suspensions, such as fruit purees, that look very cool. The sphere is formed by a chemical reaction that creates a gelled skin around the puree. This reaction occurs when sodium alginate, a compound that is extracted from brown seaweed (a kind of kelp), comes in contact with calcium ions. A sodium alginate molecule has two trailing chains of sugar molecules. The calcium ions are caught between the chains, causing the material to gel and form a skin around the puree. This gel has no flavor.

MATERIALS & EQUIPMENT

- 1,000 ml bottled water

- 5 grams sodium alginate (you can buy this online or from a restaurant supply store)

- 1 cup peeled fresh ripe mango chunks

- ½ cup coconut water or orange juice

- 1 tablespoon sugar, or more to taste

- 5 grams calcium lactate (you can buy it online or in a health food store)

- a blender

- a gram scale (to measure the sodium alginate and calcium lactate)

- 2 large glass bowls

- plastic wrap

- measuring cups and spoons

- a hemispheric mold (such as the plastic egg holder from a refrigerator or half a Styrofoam egg carton)

- a saucepan (optional)

- a Celsius lab thermometer (you can buy online)

- a slotted spoon

PROCEDURE

1   Put the water into the blender. Start the blender slowly. Add the sodium alginate to the swirling water. Beat well. Pour the mixture into a large glass bowl. Cover with plastic wrap and refrigerate overnight so that all the air bubbles in the mixture disappear.

2   Wash out the blender. Put the mangoes, coconut water or orange juice, sugar (put in more if you like it sweeter), and calcium lactate in the blender and puree. The mixture should be thick like heavy cream so that it can be poured.

3   Pour the mango puree into the mold cups. Each cup should hold about a tablespoon of puree. Cover with plastic wrap and put in the freezer.

4   The next day, take out the alginate bath and heat it in a microwave oven (or in a saucepan on the stove) until it is 65°C (150°F). You want it very warm but not boiling.

5   Prepare another warm bath of plain water in another large glass bowl to rinse your "yolks."

6   Pop out a frozen mango puree hemisphere and put it into the warm alginate bath. Start with one. If you add more, do not let them touch one another as they will stick together. Let them sit in the bath

for about 4 minutes. Use a slotted spoon to transfer them to the plain water bath. After they are rinsed, they may be stored in a small bowl in the refrigerator until ready to be served. Serve several "yolks" in a small bowl with whipped cream as dessert.

OBSERVATIONS

The warm alginate bath starts melting the frozen puree, but heat is not needed to form the skin around the puree. Freezing the puree keeps it together long enough for the gel to form. As the rest of the puree melts, the blob becomes a sphere, which is nature's most efficient shape because it contains the greatest volume of liquid for the smallest surface area. No other three-dimensional shape does this. It is why the sun, the moon, the planets, and raindrops are all spheres. The alginate bath has a much higher *specific gravity* than water and supports the weight of the mango sphere as it develops its skin. Specific gravity is a measure of whether something will float in fresh water. Salt water has a higher specific gravity than pure water; that's why you are more buoyant in seawater.

You can make spheres like this from other mixtures such as yogurt, tomato juice, or strawberry juice. You can try making them without freezing by dropping a tablespoonful into an alginate bath that has stood long enough for all the bubbles to have disappeared. It does not need to be heated for the reaction to take place. Just make sure the liquid contains enough calcium lactate to react with the sodium alginate.

One problem with the mango egg yolks is that they really do look like raw egg yolks, and that's not what we normally eat for dessert. You can use molecular gastronomy techniques to make a milk/sugar mixture look like the white of a fried egg and put the mango egg yolk on it to complete the picture. Even so, many people won't like eating something that looks like a fried egg for dessert although it tastes like a dessert. This is an interesting aspect of how the appearance of a food influences our enjoyment of it. It is definitely an area for scientific study.

NOTES

PLANTS WE EAT

All living things need a constant supply of energy in order to stay alive. The source of this energy is food combining with oxygen. The oxidation of food (sugar is an example) is the same basic overall reaction as that of fuel combining with oxygen to produce a fire. (There is, of course, a big difference that I'll tell you about in a minute.) Here's an equation that shows the similarity between the reactions:

sugar (fuel) + oxygen → carbon dioxide + water + energy (fire)

When a fuel burns, the released energy is rapid and uncontrolled. In living things, there are many steps in the oxidation of food, and the energy is released in a carefully controlled manner so that it can be used for the various activities of living.

Scientists can measure the amount of energy that can be released from different kinds of food as heat energy. They put preweighed amounts of food in a special instrument called a *calorimeter*. The food is burned with oxygen, and the heat energy given off by the reaction raises the temperature of the water outside the chamber where the food is burning. The change in the temperature of the water is a measure of the amount of energy in the food. This heat is measured in *calories*. If you look in most general cookbooks, you can find a table that lists the calories in different foods. Fats have the most calories and proteins have the least. (You can find instructions for building your own calorimeter in chapter 11, page 226–231.)

CALORIMETER

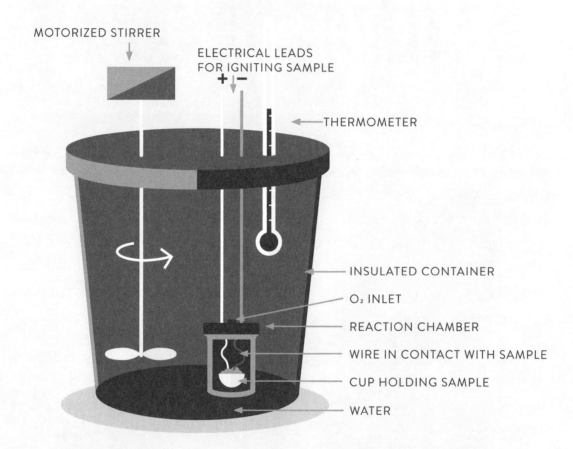

We use the energy we get from food for moving and thinking and responding to the world. Energy from food goes into building new molecules of protein and carbohydrates in our bodies. Any leftover energy not used for these activities is used to build fat molecules.

The average growing kid needs between 2,600 and 3,000 calories a day. If you eat more calories than this and don't do enough to use them up, you will gain weight.

So all living things need food. Some eat plants, some eat animals, some eat both, creating a food chain linking all forms of life to one another. The question is: What organisms are at the bottom of the food chain? These living things must be able to get energy from some source other than feeding on other living things, and they must be able to convert this energy into a substance that is food for themselves. On our planet, the bottom of the food chain is green plants.

Green plants produce their own food through a chemical reaction that is the reverse of the reaction in our bodies when we oxidize sugar:

$$carbon\ dioxide + water + energy \rightarrow sugar + oxygen$$

The outside source of energy for this reaction is sunlight. Carbon dioxide is present in air, and water is present in soil. The green pigment *chlorophyll* gives plants the ability to make sugar with these raw materials. This process of food manufacturing is called photosynthesis, which means "putting together with light."

Plants use the sugar produced during photosynthesis to make proteins, other carbohydrates, and oils. So when animals eat plants, they get energy that originally came from the sun. The importance of green plants to all other forms of life on earth is clear. Without them, we could not survive.

The experiments in this chapter will show you some of the ways plants procure the essential ingredients for photosynthesis.

RAW VEGETABLE SALAD
HOW PLANTS TAKE IN WATER

The roots of a plant have several jobs. Most roots anchor a plant to the ground. Some roots, such as carrots, also store food made in the plant's leaves. But their most important job is to absorb water from the soil.

Look at the tip of a fresh carrot that has not been trimmed or packaged. The main root, the carrot itself, becomes very slender at the tip, and there are many small roots sticking out from it. Look at these smaller roots with a magnifying glass. There are many tiny branches off each rootlet that increase the surface area of the root so more water can be absorbed. If you can't get an untrimmed carrot, put a fresh carrot, tip down, in a glass of water. It will develop new rootlets in a few days.

Water is absorbed into roots by a process called *osmosis*. In osmosis, water passes through a thin sheet of living material called a cell *membrane*. Cell membranes have holes in them that are larger than water molecules.

If the holes in cell membranes are bigger than water molecules, how come water flows *into* roots and stays there when it could just as easily flow *out*? Do the next experiment and discover the answer.

MATERIALS & EQUIPMENT

- a large carrot
- water
- salt
- a vegetable peeler
- 2 bowls
- 2 spoons

PROCEDURE

1 Peel the carrot. (Be sure to move the peeler away from your fingers.) Use the peeler to make strips of carrot.

2 Divide the strips between two bowls and add enough water to each bowl to completely cover the strips. Put about a tablespoon of salt into one of the bowls and stir. The water should taste very salty. Stir the second bowl of carrot strips with the other spoon that doesn't have salt on it.

3 Let the carrot strips soak for several hours. From time to time, take a strip from each bowl and bend and taste it to see how crisp it is.

OBSERVATIONS

Which carrot strips are crisper? Which carrots have absorbed water and which have lost water?

The direction water flows in roots depends on the minerals

dissolved in the water. When more minerals are inside the roots than in soil water, water flows into the roots, making them firm and crisp. When there are more minerals in the soil water than in roots' cells, water flows out of the roots, making them wilted and soft.

You can do many variations of this experiment with other vegetables. Thin slices of cucumber work especially well. Try different amounts of salt to see how fast wilting occurs. Find out if wilting occurs more quickly in warm (not hot) water than in cold water.

You can make a salad with all the vegetables from this experiment. Chill, then drain, the vegetables. Make a dressing of sour cream and chopped fresh dill or parsley, or try the vinaigrette from chapter 3 (see pages 38–40).

STRIPED CELERY SNACK
HOW WATER MOVES UP STEMS

One of the important jobs of plant stems is to carry water from the roots to the leaves. You can see how this happens with a stalk of celery and some food coloring.

MATERIALS & EQUIPMENT

- celery stalks
- water
- red food coloring
- 2 glasses
- a vegetable peeler
- a knife
- a plastic sandwich bag

PROCEDURE 1

1 Trim the bottom of a stalk of celery to make an even, freshly cut bottom. Put it in a glass half full of water with several drops of red food coloring added.

2 When the water has moved all the way up the stem, use a vegetable peeler to shave away the outer surface of the celery.

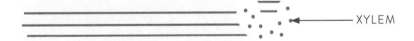

XYLEM

OBSERVATIONS

Which parts of the stem have the most food coloring? The long strands that carry water are called the *xylem*. Xylem is made of hollow cells that form a pipeline from roots to leaves. You can see where the xylem is in celery by cutting across the stalk.

PROCEDURE 2

Repeat this experiment using 2 stalks of celery. One stalk should be quite leafy and the other should have no leaves.

OBSERVATIONS

In which stalk does the water reach the top of the stem first?

PROCEDURE 3

For this experiment, use 2 leafy stalks of celery. Put one glass with its celery stalk in the sunlight and keep the other in the shade, covering the celery with a small plastic bag.

OBSERVATIONS

In which stalk does the water rise more quickly? How do your findings support the theory that the speed with which water rises in plants is a result of how fast water evaporates from the leaves?

You can eat the celery when you have finished your experiments. It's good with some peanut butter or cream cheese spread down the middle.

Try putting other vegetables in colored water. See if you can find the xylem in white radishes, scallions, and carrots. Choose a dark-colored dye that will show up against the color of the vegetables.

SPINACH
COLOR CHANGES IN CHLOROPHYLL

Spinach is a treat for many food lovers. But if you don't love spinach, perhaps it's because it was overcooked when you had it. When overcooked, spinach is a limp, unappetizing gray-green.

Fresh spinach, on the other hand, is a beautiful rich green. When it is first put in boiling water, this green brightens as gases in the cells are forced out by heating. Properly cooked spinach should be served just after it turns bright green. If you keep on cooking it, the spinach becomes grayer and grayer. Cooking releases certain acids in spinach that change the color of chlorophyll.

The amount of acid that is released during cooking is very small. It would be possible to keep spinach a bright green if this acid could be removed as soon as it was released into the cooking water. A pinch of baking soda added to the cooking water will react with the acid and "neutralize" it. (Try this to see if it works.) Baking soda, however, makes vegetables mushy, so it is not often used.

When chemists want to prevent a solution from becoming too acidic or basic, they use another kind of solution called a *buffer*. Buffers can absorb any acidic or basic molecules, removing them from a solution as soon as they are released into it. Of course, many buffers used in laboratories are not suitable for eating. But one substance we do eat that can act as a buffer is milk.

Is it possible to preserve the color of spinach by cooking it in milk? Do the next experiment to find out.

MATERIALS & EQUIPMENT

- 1 cup milk
- 1 cup water
- several fresh, washed spinach leaves
- a measuring cup
- 2 saucepans
- a slotted spoon
- a white plate

PROCEDURE

1   Put the milk in one saucepan and the water in the other. Warm the liquids over low heat.

2   When they begin to simmer, drop a few leaves of spinach into each pan, reserving one raw leaf. Keep the temperature low so the milk simmers but doesn't boil. Cook the spinach for 4 to 5 minutes. Turn off the heat and let the spinach stay in the hot liquids for another few minutes.

3   Use a slotted spoon to transfer the spinach to a white plate and compare the colors of the cooked spinach leaves to each other and to the raw spinach leaf.

OBSERVATIONS

Have the colors changed after cooking? Which seems grayer, the spinach cooked in water or the spinach cooked in milk?

Choose either milk or water to cook the rest of the spinach. Season with salt, pepper, and butter to serve.

BOILED WINTER SQUASH
A STUDY OF CELLULOSE

The experiment you did to show how water gets into plants also showed how water is important for support. Without water, plants become wilted and limp. But in addition to water, plants contain a carbohydrate called cellulose that plays an important role in the supporting structure of a plant.

The soft *protoplasm*, the living material of each plant cell, is surrounded by a cell wall made up mainly of cellulose. Cellulose is firmer than protoplasm, and the cell walls help to support a plant against the force of gravity.

Like starches, cellulose is made of chains of sugar molecules linked together. Cellulose would be a good source of food for us if we could digest it, but unfortunately, we can't. The sugar molecules in cellulose are linked together differently than the sugar molecules in starch. Cellulose links make the chain rigid and make it useless to us as food, because our digestive tracts have no way of breaking these links. Some animals, like cows, have microorganisms in their stomachs that can break down the links in a cellulose chain. For this reason, they can live on hay and grass. But the cellulose in the plants we eat leaves our bodies pretty much as it entered. It does, however, serve a useful function as fiber—also called roughage—which stimulates our digestive tracts.

The main reason we cook vegetables is to soften the cellulose so that it passes through our bodies more easily. The next experiment shows some of the conditions that change the rate at which cellulose softens during cooking.

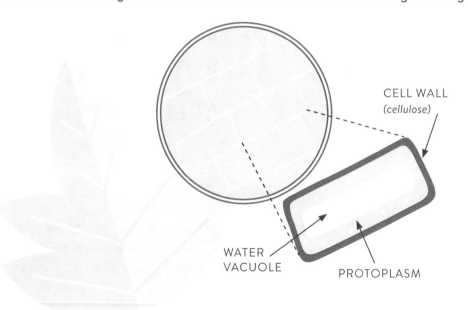

CELL WALL
(cellulose)

WATER
VACUOLE

PROTOPLASM

MATERIALS & EQUIPMENT

- a small butternut or other hard winter squash
- water
- 1 teaspoon vinegar
- ½ teaspoon baking soda

- a vegetable peeler
- a large sharp knife
- a cutting board
- a spoon

- 3 saucepans
- measuring spoons
- a slotted spoon
- a fork

PROCEDURE

1   Peel the squash with the vegetable peeler, then cut it in half the long way. Be prepared: it will be hard to cut. Scrape out the seeds and pith with a spoon. Cut the squash into 1-inch cubes, trying to keep them a similar size.

2   Divide the squash cubes among three saucepans and add enough water to each to cover the squash. Add the vinegar to one pan and the baking soda to another. The third pan, containing only water, is a control.

3   Bring the water in each pan to a boil over medium heat and let it boil while you make your observations.

4   Every few minutes, remove a piece of squash from each pan with a slotted spoon. Test it for softness by trying to mash it with a fork.

OBSERVATIONS

Which squash becomes soft first? Does cooking squash in acid speed up the rate of softening cellulose?

When all the squash is cooked, drain it and then mash it with a potato masher or an electric mixer. The squash is good plain, but even better if you add 2 tablespoons butter, 2 tablespoons brown sugar, and a dash of salt and pepper.

As you might expect, the length of cooking time for vegetables depends on the amount of cellulose in the plant. Leafy vegetables, such as spinach, do not contain much cellulose and need only be cooked for a few minutes. Artichokes, on the other hand, are high in cellulose and must be cooked quite a while to get soft. Design an experiment to check this out.

CHOP SUEY
HOW BEANS SPROUT

One of the main sources of food for people is seeds. Cereal grains, corn, rice, and beans are all seeds. Every seed is a remarkable package. It appears to be very simple. Yet it contains the cells that will become a plant and all the food needed for the baby plant to get a good start. Seeds are able to go through long periods of dryness and extreme cold and still burst with new life when conditions are right.

You can easily create the right conditions for sprouting seeds in your own kitchen.

MATERIALS & EQUIPMENT

- ¼ cup dried beans, such as lentils, lima beans, kidney beans, or black-eyed peas

- water

- a bowl

- a colander

- a clean, unglazed pot (a new flowerpot is good)

- a saucer to cover the pot

PROCEDURE

1   Put the beans in a bowl and cover with water. Let them soak overnight. As the starch in the beans absorbs the water, the beans will swell.

2   The next day, moisten the inside of a new flowerpot with water. Drain the beans in a colander and put them in the flowerpot. In order for beans to sprout, they must be kept moist but not wet. Cover the pot with the saucer and put it in a closet.

3 Check the beans every day. If they appear dry or develop the unpleasant smell of fermenting beans, wash them by running water over them in a colander and drain them well. Rinse out the flowerpot before you return the beans to it.

OBSERVATIONS

The first structure to grow from a seed is the root. This anchors the seedling to the ground and makes sure that there will be a continuous supply of water for the growing plant. Beans have two seed leaves that contain stored food. (Do these contain chlorophyll when they first emerge?) When beans sprout in soil, these thick leaves are pushed up through the soil and become green. They make food until the thinner foliage leaves develop and take over the job. Then the seed leaves shrivel and die.

FOR FURTHER STUDY

There are many experiments you can do to see how different conditions affect the sprouting of seeds. Put some soaked seeds in the refrigerator and compare them with seeds sprouting at room temperature. Find out if light and darkness affect sprouting. Take a few seeds just when the roots appear and put them between two pieces of moist folded paper towels held together by paper clips. Keep the towels moist and prop them up so the roots are pointed upward, opposite to the pull of gravity. Watch to see how these roots grow over several days.

Add the sprouts to canned or frozen chop suey and heat just until hot. They should be crisp and delicious.

POPCORN

MEASURING MOISTURE IN SEEDS

No matter how dry seeds seem to be, all seeds contain a tiny bit of water that keeps the cells alive until conditions are favorable for sprouting. It is this tiny bit of water that makes popcorn poppable.

When a kernel of popping corn is heated quickly, the water inside the kernel becomes steam, a gas that exerts pressure strong enough to burst the tough seed coat. Once free of its container, the gas expands rapidly, causing the soft starch in the seed to puff up into millions of tiny rigid-walled bubbles. This white, Styrofoam-like material is what we think of as popcorn. If you look carefully at a popped popcorn, you can find the remains of the burst seed coat. In effect, popping turns the seed inside out!

What happens to the popability of popcorn when you change the amount of moisture in the seed? Do the next experiment to find out.

MATERIALS & EQUIPMENT

- 1½ cups fresh popping corn

- water

- 9 tablespoons vegetable oil

- measuring cups and spoons

- a cookie sheet

- a jar with a cover

- a hot-air popper or a deep pot with a lid

- 3 identical 8-ounce glass tumblers

- a ruler

1. INTACT KERNEL

2. SEED COAT RUPTURES

3. MOISTURE/GAS EXPANDING DUE TO HEAT

PROCEDURE

1 Preheat the oven to 200°F (93°C). Put ½ cup of the popping corn in a single layer on a cookie sheet and bake for 2 hours. (Does any corn pop during the heating? If not, why not?)

2 Put another ½ cup of the popping corn in a jar. Add 1 tablespoon of water. Put the cover on the jar and shake it so that the water coats all the seeds. Let the jar stand overnight. Every few hours, give the jar a shake to redistribute the water. (You can let it stand without shaking while you sleep.)

3 The next day, pop the ½ cup dried corn, the ½ cup wet corn, and the ½ cup untreated corn in three separate batches. A hot-air popper works best, but if you don't have a popper, you can use a deep pot with a lid. Put about 3 tablespoon of vegetable oil on the bottom of the pot and add 2 kernels of popcorn from one batch. Heat the oil over high heat until the 2 kernels pop. Then add the rest of that batch of corn, cover, and shake over lower heat until the popping stops. Remove the popcorn from the heat. Repeat for the other two batches.

4 Count 50 popped kernels from the first group into a glass and measure how high the popcorn reaches. This is a measure of the volume of the popped corn. Measure 50 popped kernels from the other two batches in the same way and compare. Which corn has the largest volume? Which has the smallest?

4. SEED COAT CURLS BACK AND BECOMES HEART OF POPPED CORN

OBSERVATIONS

How does the volume of the heated corn compare to the volume of the moistened corn and the untreated corn? The amount of moisture in popcorn is crucial to the size of the finished product. Popcorn manufacturers make it their business to know just how much water is needed.

Popcorn is harvested when the moisture is 16 to 19 percent of the weight of a kernel. The optimal moisture for popping is 13 to 14.5 percent. So the harvested corn has to dry out a little before it is ready to be packaged and sold. Popped corn is more than 25 percent larger than unpopped, and there are two basic shapes for popped corn—butterfly and mushroom. (Butterfly is the more common type, sold in movie theaters; mushroom is used in Cracker Jack.) Popcorn pops when the steam inside reaches 347°F (175°C) and the pressure is nine times atmospheric pressure or 135 pounds per square inch. At this point the seed coat ruptures, and the internal starch rapidly expands into bubbles that solidify as they cool.

There are other seeds you can try to pop. Compare expensive popcorn with inexpensive brands. Try popping sweet corn seeds. Put a little oil in the bottom of a deep pot with a lid. Shake the seeds as you heat them. When I popped sweet corn, I got corn nuts. Another seed that pops is amaranth, which you can buy at health food stores. Pop amaranth in a pot without oil. Use a magnifying glass to examine the popped amaranth.

Microwave popcorn also lends itself to some experiments . . . coming up in the next chapter.

notes

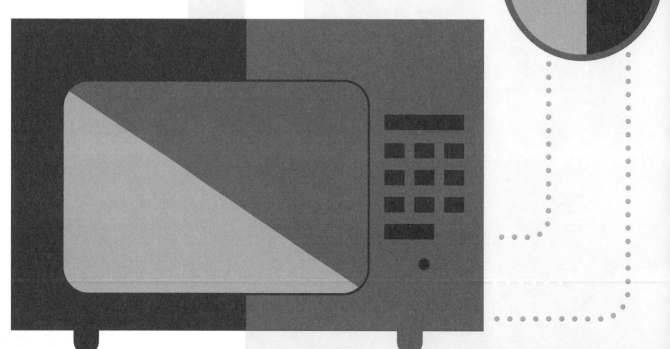

MICROWAVE COOKING

There are thousands of professional food scientists who make a living working on science experiments you can eat. Since this book was first published, one of the biggest challenges for these food scientists has become the microwave oven.

Microwaves are a form of energy that occurs in nature in sunlight as well as in the light from all other stars. Microwaves are one kind of *electromagnetic radiation*. Others are visible light, radio waves, X rays, gamma rays, and cosmic rays.

When microwaves come into contact with water molecules, they make the molecules twist their position. Microwave ovens produce a high concentration of microwave radiation, alternating its direction back and forth between 915 and 2,450 million times per second. Water molecules bombarded by microwaves twist back and forth that many times. They move! Increased motion of water molecules becomes heat energy that can cook food. Since the microwaves act directly on the water in food, and not on the container or the air in the oven, the food heats up while the oven itself stays cool. Cooking containers get hot as heat is transferred from the food to the container.

Microwaves in an oven are generated by a device called a *magnetron*, which uses a magnet to make electrons travel rapidly in a circular path. The circling electrons generate microwaves that pass through a wave guide to the top of the oven, where the waves strike a rotating "stirrer" that looks something like a propeller. As the microwaves reflect off the stirrer, they are distributed in all directions into the space of the oven. The waves also bounce off the oven walls. Ideally, the microwaves should be evenly distributed throughout the oven so that food cooks evenly. But in reality, even with stirrers, all microwave ovens have hot spots. Putting food on a rotating carousel is one way to make sure it cooks more evenly. You can make a map of the hot spots in your microwave oven with the next experiment.

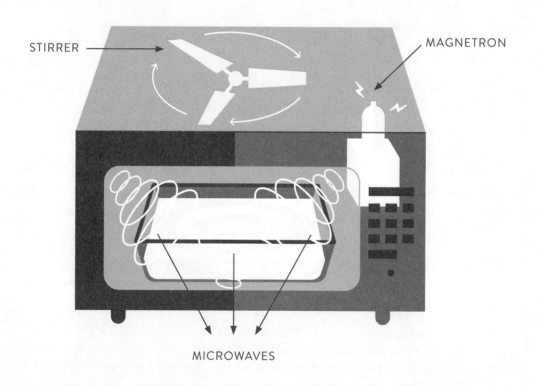

STIRRER

MAGNETRON

MICROWAVES

HONEY CAKE

A MAP OF MICROWAVE HOT SPOTS

A mixture of honey and flour will caramelize to show the places where the microwaves are focused.

MATERIALS & EQUIPMENT

- 1 cup cake flour

- 1 teaspoon baking soda

- 1 egg

- 1 cup honey

- nonstick cooking spray

- measuring cups and spoons

- a bowl

- a big spoon

- a 9" x 13" glass baking dish

- 1 egg white

- heat-sensitive fax paper

PROCEDURE 1

1   Measure the flour and baking soda into the bowl. Stir in the egg, then the honey to make a smooth mixture.

2   Spray the baking dish with nonstick cooking spray. Pour the batter into the baking dish and smooth out the surface so there is a thin layer that completely covers the bottom.

3   If your microwave has a revolving tray, remove it and then microwave the honey mixture on high for 7 minutes.

OBSERVATIONS

Notice the pattern of browning on the top of the cake. This shows where the microwaves are focused in the oven to form hotter areas. The brownness is due to the caramelizing of the honey. Is the browning on top only, or does it go through the thickness of the cake? What does the browning tell you about the way the inside of the cake is heated compared to the outside? If your microwave has a revolving tray, try cooking another honey cake using the tray. How effective is this method for counteracting the hot spots in your oven?

I cannot recommend this cake for its taste. Microwaving seems to develop the gluten in wheat flour, and it also causes a gummy material to form on the bottom of the cake. You might want to experiment to see if you can improve the recipe by adding butter and substituting another kind of flour for the wheat flour.

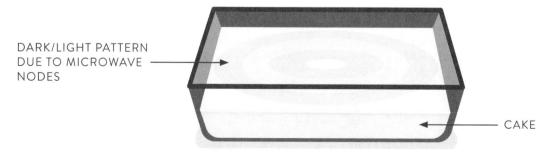

DARK/LIGHT PATTERN
DUE TO MICROWAVE
NODES

CAKE

PROCEDURE 2

Spray the pan with nonstick cooking spray and cover the bottom of a glass baking dish with egg white. Watch to see which areas coagulate first. The egg white is edible, but it's even less tasty than the honey cake. Don't let it heat for more than 7 minutes.

PROCEDURE 3

You can still get thermal, heat-sensitive fax paper. Heat a sheet for about 7 minutes. There's no way "nuked" fax paper can be a science experiment you can eat, but it does give you a map of your microwave's hot spots.

BOILING MICROWAVED WATER WITHOUT HEAT

In an ordinary oven, heat penetrates food from the outside in. Microwaves can penetrate about an inch into whatever you're heating. All the water molecules respond wherever they are struck, so if you boil water in a cup with a 2-inch diameter, the inside molecules are heated at the same time as the outside molecules (except for the hot spots). This accounts for the speed of microwave heating, the main advantage of a microwave oven.

Water boils when the molecules move fast enough to escape from the surface into the air. When you boil water in a pot, the heat source is at the bottom, and the molecules at the bottom move faster than those at the top. In early stages of heating, the molecules lose some of this motion as they encounter cooler molecules on their rise to the top. Boiling is when bubbles of water vapor collect on the bottom of the pot and rise to the surface.

You can bring water that has been heated in a microwave to a boil after you remove it from the microwave oven by adding sugar.

MATERIALS & EQUIPMENT

- 1 cup water

- ½ teaspoon sugar

- a 1-cup Pyrex measuring cup

- measuring spoons

PROCEDURE

1   Fill a Pyrex measuring cup with the water and microwave it on high for 2 minutes and 30 seconds.

2   Remove the cup from the microwave. Add the sugar all at once, but don't stir. Watch a rush of bubbles come to the surface about a second after you add sugar.

OBSERVATIONS

When you boil water by microwave, the entire container is evenly heated. Molecules capable of escaping can be found in the middle of the liquid with cooler molecules around the edges, depending on where the hot spots of your oven are located. If you heat it long enough, microwave-heated water will boil. But if you remove it before you see bubbles, you have a lot of water that has reached the boiling point but has not yet escaped into the air. When you add sugar, the sugar crystals act as points of disturbance that bubbles of water vapor can form around. The bubbles quickly rise to the surface. Many people have noticed this phenomenon when they reheat coffee in the microwave and then add sugar.

You can also boil water that contains ice. The trick is to put very little water in a Pyrex measuring cup with a lot of ice cubes. Water molecules are free to move when struck by microwaves, but frozen water molecules are not. Until the ice is surrounded by enough hot water to liquefy them, they remain solid.

You won't save time trying to microwave frozen soup. In fact, liquid soup can boil away before a solid block of frozen soup melts. Defrosting by microwave consists of alternating a blast of microwaves with a period of no microwaves. The heat picked up by liquid water molecules is transferred to liquefy adjacent frozen molecules during the resting period.

MICROWAVING AWAY STALENESS

As bread ages, it gets stale. The moisture in the bread evaporates, and the bread dries out. Also, as time passes, the starch in bread recrystallizes. Both of these processes cause the bread to become hard or stale. Temperature is one variable that affects staling. Bread will get stale faster at lower temperatures that are above freezing than at room temperature. So putting bread in the refrigerator can hasten its staling, not preserve it. Freezing almost completely stops staling. Can you design an experiment to test this idea?

Stale starch crystals melt at 140°F (60°C). Reheating stale bread in a toaster or the oven seems like a good solution, but heating causes even more moisture to be lost, making the bread drier. However, you can freshen stale bread in a microwave: Sprinkle it with water, wrap it in a paper towel, and heat it for 5 to 10 seconds on high.

Microwaving causes water molecules to migrate through food and condense on the surface. This tends to make the surfaces of baked goods gummy instead of crisp. Paper towels wrapped around food absorb some of the surface moisture and keep baked goods from becoming soggy. Microwave ovens destroy a crisp crust. But don't take my word for it; try it and see for yourself. The reason cakes and breads baked in microwaves don't brown is because water at their surfaces makes them too cool to brown.

You can also freshen bread in a regular oven if you sprinkle it with water, wrap it in foil, and heat it for 3 to 4 minutes.

MICROWAVE POPCORN

The heating ability of microwaves was discovered accidentally by Dr. Percy Spencer, a researcher on shortwave electromagnetic energy for the Raytheon

Company. He was visiting a laboratory that made magnetrons for radar tracking devices. He noticed that the microwaves from a magnetron melted a piece of candy in his pocket. He sent out for a bag of popcorn, which popped when he put it near the magnetron. Although many radar engineers were aware of the heating properties of microwaves, Spencer was the first to apply them to cooking food. Raytheon went on to build the first microwave ovens in 1946. And the rest, as they say, is history.

One of the most successful products designed for the microwave oven is popcorn. The key to microwaved popcorn is not in the corn but in the bag. Do the following experiments to learn more about popcorn and its amazing microwavable bag.

MATERIALS & EQUIPMENT

- a package of microwave popcorn
- ½ cup ordinary popping corn
- scissors
- waxed paper
- plastic wrap
- a measuring cup
- 2 large glass bowls
- a small sharp knife
- potholders

PROCEDURE

1   Cut open the end of a microwave popcorn bag. Empty the contents onto a piece of waxed paper. Notice that the kernels are embedded in a solid, fatty material.

2   Put about ½ cup of the embedded kernels in the bottom of a glass bowl. Seal the top with plastic wrap. Make a small slit in the middle of the plastic wrap with a knife to vent.

3   Put the ordinary popping corn in another glass bowl. Cover this bowl with plastic wrap as well and make a vent.

4   Microwave each bowl of corn separately on high for 4 minutes. Remove the bowls with potholders. Carefully pull off the plastic wrap. **Warning:** There is a lot of steam trapped in the bowls. Loosen the wrap on the side of the bowl farthest from you and pull it back slowly. This way your hands and arms will not be exposed to the steam.

OBSERVATIONS

In each sample, see how many unpopped kernels (UPKs) there are. There are about 200 kernels in ½ cup of unpopped popcorn, so you can calculate the percentage of UPKs with the following formula:

(Number of UPKs ÷ 200) × 100 = the percent of UPKs

The solid fatty material that the microwave popcorn comes in converts microwave energy into heat energy and is in direct contact with the kernels. Since the kernels are not agitated as they are in an air popper or when you shake a pot over a flame, the fatty material makes sure that the kernels are all heated fairly evenly. But microwave popcorn still has a higher percentage of UPKs than popcorn popped in oil. Can you design an experiment to check out this idea?

The popcorn that is popped dry still pops, but there is usually an even higher percentage of UPKs, and there is usually a higher percentage of kernels that are not completely popped.

Food engineers went to work: How could the number of UPKs be reduced? They discovered that the key was not the popcorn but the design of the bag. For more kernels to pop, you need to concentrate the heat. You are instructed to place the bag in the oven with a particular side down. Cut the bag close to the center panel that is supposed to rest on the oven floor. Tear it toward the center. Notice that the bag is made of three layers. The outer layer is a grease-resistant paper. The inner layer is a grease-proof paper. The middle layer is a polyester film embedded with a light layer of aluminum. The metallic film absorbs microwaves and becomes hot, thus concentrating the heat in one place so it can be conducted by the fatty material directly to the kernels. An interesting aside: The Stealth bomber is coated with a ceramic embedded with aluminum that absorbs the microwaves of radar and allows the plane to avoid being tracked.

Popcorn also needs space. The problem the engineers faced was how to design a package that could be compact on the supermarket shelf yet be large enough to give the popcorn room to pop. The answer is in the expandable, pleated bag. If the volume of a container is restricted, the popcorn will not pop as large. Can you design an experiment to test this idea?

NOTES

MICROBES

Ever clean out the refrigerator and discover that some once-appetizing foods are now mushy, fuzzy, or foul smelling? Now imagine what our ancestors, who had no refrigerators, had to deal with. Your senses find rotting food unpleasant for good reason: It can make you sick.

Cooking was one way our human ancestors tried to delay spoilage. Strong spices and herbs were used to mask the flavor of tainted meat and fish. It is not surprising that the strongest spices, like pepper, chili, and curry, were first used in warm climates, where food spoils more quickly than in colder parts of the world.

But not all the changes in food left to stand were unpleasant. Milk could be made into cheese, grape juice could become wine, flour-and-water paste developed bubbles and became bread when baked. These pleasant changes became ways of preserving food also. Cheese and wine could be consumed months after they were prepared. Dry grain could be stored without rotting to be ground into flour at some later time. In days when there were no such things as canning, freezing, or refrigerating food, cheese, bread, and wine were a protection against famine. They were among the most important foods of early civilizations.

The change in grape juice as it became wine was so well known that it had its own name, *fermentation*, meaning "to boil." As grape juice ferments, tiny bubbles form that are similar to the bubbles in boiling liquids, except that the grape juice is not hot. Although people have known how to make wine for centuries, it wasn't until the middle of the nineteenth century, when something went wrong with the wine industry of France, that we began to understand what caused grape juice to ferment.

The problem was that some wine went sour as it aged. Since the spoiled wine was prepared in exactly the same way as wine that was good, the winemakers couldn't understand how the spoiling occurred. In desperation, they called in a great scientist, Louis Pasteur (1822–1895), to try to solve their problem.

Pasteur studied the wine in good vats and in spoiled vats. He found that both fermentation and wine spoilage were products of living things, *microbes*, which could be seen only with a microscope. The microbe that fermented grape juice into wine used sugar from the grapes as food and produced alcohol and carbon dioxide as waste products. The microbes that spoiled the wine used alcohol formed by the first microbes as food. It was the wastes of these second microbes that gave the wine a bad taste.

To solve the winemakers' problem, Pasteur made the following suggestion: Kill the microbes by heating the wine gently to denature the protein in the microbes but not hot enough to boil the wine (about the same temperature as boiling water). This heating process, called *pasteurization*, is a standard procedure today for killing harmful microbes in dairy products, beer, and wine.

Microbes are everywhere—in air, in water, in soil, and in our bodies. The study of microbes has touched on all aspects of human life, including agriculture, medicine, chemical products for industry, and biotechnical engineering as well as food preparation and preservation. The experiments in this chapter will show you how microbes act in some of the foods we eat.

SALLY LUNN BREAD
A STUDY OF YEAST ACTIVITY

Yeasts are one-celled plants that are distant cousins of mushrooms. Like mushrooms and other plants that do not contain chlorophyll, yeasts cannot make their own food and must get it from their surroundings. When conditions are not favorable, yeasts become inactive, only to spring to life when conditions are right.

The products of fermentation, alcohol and carbon dioxide, are of utmost importance to the winemaker and the baker. The winemaker is interested in alcohol production and the baker is interested in carbon dioxide, for it is this gas that makes bread rise.

The next experiment is designed to show what kind of food yeasts need for growth. Other essential conditions for growth—temperature and moisture—will be made as favorable as possible.

MATERIALS & EQUIPMENT

- 1 packet dry yeast
- water warmed to 110°F (43°C)
- 1 tablespoon sugar

Continued . . .

- 1 tablespoon cornstarch
- measuring cups and spoons
- a candy thermometer
- 1 tablespoon corn syrup
- 3 (6-ounce) glasses
- 3 spoons
- a large pot

PROCEDURE

1 Dissolve the yeast in ½ cup of 110°F (43°C) water. Divide the yeast mixture equally among three glasses.

2 Put the sugar in the first glass, the corn syrup in the next glass, and the cornstarch in the third glass. Stir each glass with a different spoon.

3 Set up a warm-water bath for the yeast in a large pot. Put enough 110°F (43°C) water in the pot to come about halfway up the sides of the glasses containing the yeast mixture, as shown in the illustration. Be sure not to let any of the water from the bath get into the glasses. The bathwater will remain warm long enough to generate active fermentation.

4 Measure fermentation by the size of the bubbles in the foam and the rate at which they form.

OBSERVATIONS

The material a microbe uses as food is called a *substrate*. Which substrate in your experiment starts being fermented first? Which substrate has the steadiest rate of fermentation? Can you smell the alcohol produced by fermentation?

In baked goods, the yeast uses glucose as its principal substrate. Glucose is the principal food of yeast used for baking. When yeast comes into contact with glucose, fermentation begins immediately. Glucose is present in corn syrup. Yeast can also get glucose from sucrose (table sugar) and starch, but it takes longer to get going, as sucrose and starch have to be broken down into simpler sugars before fermentation can occur. How do your findings support this idea?

Now use your experiment to make bread.

MATERIALS & EQUIPMENT

- ½ cup milk

- 1 stick (½ cup) butter

- all the mixtures from the preceding experiment

- about 3½ cups flour

- 1 teaspoon salt

- 3 eggs

- a medium saucepan

- a candy thermometer

- a large bowl

- an electric mixer

- a damp, clean dish towel

- an 8" x 4" x 2" loaf pan

- a sharp knife

- a wire rack

- butter or cooking spray

PROCEDURE

1 Put the milk and butter in a saucepan and heat until the milk is about 85°F (29°C). Don't let the milk get too hot, or you will kill the yeast.

2 Pour all three glasses from your experiment into a large bowl and add the milk-and-butter mixture.

3 Add about a cup of the flour and the salt to the liquids. Mix on low speed with an electric mixer. When all the flour is moistened, beat the batter for about 2 minutes on medium speed to develop the gluten protein. (If you're wondering about developing gluten, check out the experiment on page 100.)

4 Beat in the eggs and add another cup of the flour. Finally, add enough of the remaining flour to make a stiff batter that can still be stirred.

5 Cover the bowl with a moist, clean dish towel and place in a warm spot to rise. While the batter is rising, grease the loaf pan (you can use butter or cooking spray) and sprinkle a few tablespoons of flour on the pan. Shake the pan so that the flour evenly coats the greased surfaces and dump out any extra flour.

6 Let the batter rise until it doubles in size—about an hour. Then punch it down with your fist. What gives the batter its stretchy consistency? Examine the air pockets in the batter. Are they evenly distributed? Are there larger air pockets near the source of heat?

7 Beat the batter with the mixer again for about 30 seconds. Put the batter in the loaf pan, cover with the dish towel, and let it rise again until it has doubled in size (about an hour). Preheat the oven to 325°F (163°C).

8 Bake the bread for about 50 minutes. It is done when the sides of the bread draw slightly away from the sides of the pan. Run a sharp knife around the bread as soon as you take it from the oven. Remove the bread from the pan and let it cool on a wire rack. Sally Lunn bread is best served while still warm.

PRETZELS

INHIBITING YEAST ACTION

When you add other chemicals to the yeast environment, you can affect fermentation. The next experiment shows how.

MATERIALS & EQUIPMENT

- 1 packet dry yeast

- water warmed to 110°F (43°C)

- ½ teaspoon sugar

- ¼ teaspoon salt

- a candy thermometer

- measuring cups and spoons

- 3 identical small glasses

- 3 spoons

- a large pot

PROCEDURE

1 Dissolve the yeast in 1 cup of 110°F (43°C) water. Divide the yeast solution equally among the three glasses.

2 Put ¼ teaspoon of the sugar in the first glass. Put the remaining ¼ teaspoon sugar and the salt in the second glass. Leave the third glass without substrate as a control. Stir each glass with a different spoon.

3 Make a warm-water bath as you did for the previous experiment. Put the three glasses in the water bath and watch for fermentation activity.

OBSERVATIONS

Which glass has the most activity? Which glass has the least? Does salt inhibit yeast activity? How can you tell?

Use this experiment to make pretzels.

MATERIALS & EQUIPMENT

- yeast mixtures from the previous experiment
- about 4½ cups flour
- 1 egg yolk, beaten
- 1 tablespoon water
- coarse (kosher) salt
- a big spoon
- a clean, damp dish towel

- vegetable oil
- a small bowl
- 2 large bowls
- a whisk or fork
- a cookie sheet
- a pastry brush

PROCEDURE

1 Put the contents of the previous experiment in a large bowl. Add between 4 and 4½ cups flour. Mix to form a stiff dough.

2 Knead the dough on a floured surface for about 8 minutes. Kneading develops the gluten, which is the only protein that supports pretzels (Sally Lunn bread has milk and eggs to help do this job). To knead, dump the dough out onto a floured surface and rub some flour on your hands to keep them from sticking to the dough. Fold over, toward you, the side of the dough farthest from you. Push the fold into the rest of the dough with the heel of your hand. Give the dough a quarter turn and repeat the motion. Dough that has been properly kneaded is no longer sticky but smooth and elastic.

3 Oil a large bowl and put in the kneaded dough, turning the dough so that it becomes slightly oiled and will not dry out. Cover the dough with a clean, damp dish towel. Let it rise in a warm place until it doubles in size.

4 While the dough is rising, grease the cookie sheet and make the egg mixture: In a small bowl or custard cup, beat the yolk and water using a whisk or a fork.

5 When the dough is finished rising, punch it down with your fist. Break off balls of dough and roll them between your hands into long ropes. Then shape them into pretzels and put them on the cookie sheet. You can make many different shapes.

6 Use a pastry brush to paint each pretzel with the egg yolk mixture. Sprinkle the pretzels with coarse salt.

7 Preheat the oven to 475°F (246°C). Let the pretzels rise again in a warm place until they have almost doubled in size. Then bake them for about 10 minutes or until the pretzels are firm and golden brown.

A COMPARISON OF YOGURT CULTURES

Bacteria are one-celled microbes that are smaller than yeast. Bacteria, like yeast, must also get food from their surroundings, and they can use many substances as food. Some even live on such unappetizing materials as rubber and petroleum. The bacteria you'll be experimenting with live on milk.

Milk is a mixture of many substances—water, proteins, fats, and a sugar, found only in milk, known as *lactose*. Certain bacteria feed on lactose and give off *lactic acid* as a waste product.

As lactic-acid bacteria grow, more and more lactic acid collects, giving milk a sour taste, typical of acids. What is even more striking than the change in taste is the change in texture. Lactic acid causes milk proteins to become denatured, making the milk thicker and thicker. Such cultured milk, called yogurt, has a nutty, sour taste and a custardy texture.

Frozen yogurt has become a popular dessert. But the first frozen yogurts were simply frozen versions of traditional yogurt, and they did not sell. People did not like sour ice cream. The successful versions on the market today use different strains of bacteria in the culture. Culture your own yogurt at home using two different starter cultures to see what the difference really is.

It is simple to make yogurt at home. The recipe that follows is certain to produce good results because you will be creating ideal conditions for the growth of lactic-acid bacteria.

MATERIALS & EQUIPMENT

- ½ gallon skim milk
- ½ cup commercially prepared plain yogurt
- 1 cup vanilla frozen yogurt, melted
- a saucepan

- a candy thermometer
- measuring cups
- 2 medium bowls
- 2 clean 1½-quart glass jars with covers
- 2 spoons

- labels
- a pen
- 2 dish towels
- an insulated picnic cooler

PROCEDURE

1. Warm the milk in a saucepan over low heat until a skin forms (160°F, or 71°C). This kills any bacteria that may cause the milk to spoil before the yogurt forms. Let the milk cool until it is 110°F (43°C).

2. Mix the plain yogurt and 1 cup of the warm milk in a bowl. Next, mix the melted frozen yogurt with 1 cup of the warm milk in another bowl. Divide the remaining warm milk equally between two glass jars.

3   Stir each of the starter cultures into a different jar of milk. Label the jars so you know which contains the plain yogurt starter culture and which contains the frozen yogurt starter culture.

4   Wrap each jar in a dish towel and place in the cooler. Cover the cooler and check your yogurt after about 6 hours. The yogurt is finished when it moves away from the side of the container in one piece if you tilt it. Cover and refrigerate the finished yogurt to stop the growth of the bacteria.

OBSERVATIONS

Which culture finished first? Which was more sour? How does the consistency compare? Look at the labels on the original containers of both yogurts. Which type has more ingredients? The plain yogurt uses a strain of bacteria called *Lactobacillus acidophilus*. Frozen yogurts don't usually identify the microbes they use, but it is normally a combination of *Streptococcus thermophilus* and *Lactobacillus bulgaricus* in secret proportions.

The recipe produced good results because you created ideal conditions for the growth of lactic-acid bacteria. Try making yogurt at different temperatures. Compare yogurt made with fresh whole milk, condensed milk, and powdered milk. Find out what happens when you add sugar to the milk. Use different brands of commercially prepared yogurt as starter cultures. Try using acidophilus powders of capsules from a health food store as starter cultures. See how many generations of yogurt you can produce from the yogurt you make. (This is where you use one culture you've made as a starter culture for a new batch.) Use red cabbage indicator (see page 20) to measure changes in acidity as the culture grows.

Your yogurt may be eaten plain or mixed with fresh fruit, fruit preserves, honey, maple syrup, or a small amount of defrosted concentrated orange juice.

CULTURED CREAM

Here's another experiment with *lactobacilli*. These rod-shaped microscopic organisms are ordinarily found floating in the air in an inactive, or "latent," state. When they land in some milk, they spring to life, using the sugar in milk as food. Bacteria don't get "fatter" as they take in food; instead, each organism divides in half, and their numbers increase. In this experiment you study the effects of two different starter cultures on heavy cream. The end result is a thick, rich, slightly sour cream that is quite delicious. The French call it crème fraîche.

MATERIALS & EQUIPMENT

- 1 pint heavy cream

- 1 teaspoon cultured buttermilk

- 1 teaspoon sour cream

- 2 spotlessly clean 1- to 2-cup jars with lids (peanut butter jars are good)

- measuring cup and spoons

- spoons

PROCEDURE

1   Put 1 cup (½ pint) of the heavy cream in each jar. Add the cultured buttermilk to one jar and stir. Add the sour cream to the other jar and stir with a clean spoon. (The sour cream will be lumpy and will need to be broken up so it will blend in smoothly.) Use a different spoon for each stirring operation. Taste the contents of each jar, using the spoon you stirred it with. Don't contaminate the jars by putting in a spoon that has been in your mouth. Don't let anything you have touched with your hands or mouth come in contact with the contents of the jars. Keep everything as clean as possible. Undesirable microbes can grow just as easily as lactobacilli.

2   Screw on the covers of the jars tightly. Allow them to stand in a warm place overnight. (The top of a dishwasher or other warm appliance works well.) The cream should become too thick to pour; this may take from 16 to 36 hours. The thickness of the cream is considered the "measure of ripeness" of crème fraîche.

OBSERVATIONS

Which crème fraîche is smoother? Which is more sour? Different cultures give the cream different flavors. You will probably prefer one over the other. I liked the buttermilk culture better.

Refrigerate and use within a week. Crème fraîche is especially delicious with fresh fruit and a little sugar. Try some on sliced ripe bananas and add a little brown sugar and cinnamon. Or try some on granola or another cereal.

FOR FURTHER STUDY

Try making crème fraîche with a yogurt culture; stir 1 teaspoon plain yogurt into the heavy cream. Also, try to get similar results from a yeast culture. Mix ¼ teaspoon active dry yeast with 1 tablespoon warm milk. Add the mixture to 1 cup heavy cream. Stir, put a lid on the jar, and let stand in a warm place until the cream thickens. How do the yogurt and yeast cultures taste?

Repeat the procedure to see the effect of temperature on bacterial activity. Use a single starter culture, such as yogurt or buttermilk. Set up three samples. Put one jar in the refrigerator; heat one sample to boiling in a saucepan, then pour it into a jar and leave it at room temperature; keep the third at room temperature overnight. Can you now explain why cultured milk products are sold in a refrigerated state? What effect does boiling have on lactobacilli? You can check this out further by boiling your starter culture and then adding it to new cream. Will it become crème fraîche?

COTTAGE CHEESE

WHOLE MILK VS. SKIM MILK

The basis of all cheese is milk solids, the proteins and fats in milk. Milk solids can be separated from the watery portion of milk in several ways. You can add an acid, such as lemon juice or vinegar. You can add an enzyme, such as rennet, the milk-coagulating protein derived from the stomachs of calves. It's used to make junket desserts, which used to be popular for babies. Rennet tablets can now be purchased online. And, of course, you can use a lactobacilli culture. When milk is made into cheese, the milk protein is coagulated and then separated as "curds" from the watery portion of the milk or "whey." Cottage cheese is one of the simplest fresh cheeses to prepare.

Cottage cheese has been popular with people trying to lose weight. That's because most commercial cottage cheese is made from skim milk—milk with the butterfat removed. In this experiment you make cottage cheese from skim milk and compare it with cottage cheese you make from whole milk. The question you'll be trying to answer is: Does butterfat make a difference in the texture and taste of cottage cheese curds?

Note: In any cheese-making experiment, there is a possibility that your mixture, instead of ripening, will spoil. This can happen if your equipment isn't perfectly clean, or if the temperature is too high. If your cheese smells bad or looks spoiled, **do not eat it**.

MATERIALS & EQUIPMENT

- ½ gallon fat-free (skim) milk
- ½ gallon whole milk
- cultured buttermilk
- 2 large glass or ceramic bowls or stainless steel pots (don't use aluminum or cast iron)
- measuring spoons

- spoons
- plastic wrap
- a knife
- a very large pot and a small one (stainless steel) that fits inside it—to be used as a double boiler
- a candy thermometer

- a colander
- cheesecloth
- 2 small bowls
- 2 small glasses
- heavy cream or crème fraîche (optional)

PROCEDURE

1 Allow the cartons of milk to stand, unrefrigerated, for several hours, until the milk is at room temperature. Pour the skim milk into one large bowl and the whole milk into the other. Add 3 tablespoons of buttermilk to each and stir well. Cover each bowl with plastic wrap and put the bowls in a warm place overnight.

2 The next day, the milk will be "clabbered," or like a soft custard. (Using what you learned in the Cultured Cream experiment on page 182, can you explain what causes the milk to clabber?) The milk is ready for the next step if the whey is starting to collect around the edges. If this isn't happening, it isn't "ripe" yet. Give it more time.

3   Make slices through the curds 1 inch apart. Repeat at right angles to the first slices to make a crisscross pattern, forming rough cubes.

4   The next step is to further coagulate the curds and cause them to separate from the whey. This is done by very slowly heating the curds to about 100°F (38°C) (just warm to the touch). If you heat the curds too quickly or at too high a temperature, they will become tough. Put a bowl containing the clabbered milk over a pot containing hot water. (If the bowl doesn't fit over the pot, or if it isn't heatproof, gently pour the curds and whey into a stainless steel saucepan that does fit into the larger pot.) Heat over very low heat, stirring occasionally. The heating process should take about 30 minutes. Heat until the milk is just warm to the touch.

5   Remove the curds and whey from the heat and let them cool for about 20 minutes. Meanwhile, repeat the procedure with the second batch of clabbered milk.

6   Skim off about ¼ cup of whey from the first batch of cheese into a small glass. Set aside. Line a colander with two layers of cheesecloth. Pour the curds and whey from this first batch into the cheesecloth and let drain. From time to time, lift up the cheesecloth and shake the curds to let pockets of trapped whey drain through. Bring the tops of the cheesecloth together, and twist and squeeze out the remaining whey. Put the drained curds into a small bowl. (If you wish you can rinse the curds in the cheesecloth under cool water. I didn't find this necessary.) Repeat this procedure as precisely as possible with the other batch of cheese.

OBSERVATIONS

Taste the whey samples from both batches. Are they different in appearance and taste? Taste the curds from both batches. Which are more tender? (One standard for judging the quality of cottage cheese is the tenderness of the curd.) Do you think butterfat plays a role in making a more tender curd?

Salt the curds and mix in heavy cream (or crème fraîche from the previous experiment) to taste. Refrigerate the cheese until you are ready to eat it. Cottage cheese is perishable and should be eaten within two or three days.

FOR FURTHER STUDY

Design an experiment to observe what happens when clabbered curds are heated to about 100°F (38°C).

Make cottage cheese from straight cultured buttermilk. You can also try different starter cultures, including yogurt and commercial cottage cheese. Clabber milk with an acid such as lemon juice or vinegar. Meat tenderizer (actually an enzyme called *papain*) also clabbers milk. Try making cheese with this enzyme. Rennet tablets are used to make commercial cottage cheese. You can find them online and make cheese with them.

NOTES

ENZYMES AND HORMONES

In 1897, Eduard Buchner, a German chemist, ground up some yeast cells and made an extract from them. He put this extract in grape juice and found, to his astonishment, that the grape juice still fermented. For the first time, glucose became alcohol and carbon dioxide without using living cells. The substance in Buechner's extract that caused fermentation was called *enzyme*, from the Greek roots *en* and *zyme*, meaning "leavened."

Today we think of enzymes as the molecules that control the countless numbers of chemical reactions in living organisms. The role of enzymes becomes impressive when you look closely at a few of the reactions that take place in a living thing. The oxidation of food, for example, does not burn in your body the way it burns in a calorimeter. If it did, a piece of chocolate cake containing 300 calories would raise the body temperature of a 100-pound person to about 118°F (48°C)[1], high enough to cause death. In your body, food combines with many different substances in a chain of reactions and a little energy is released with each step. Releasing the energy from oxidation in a controlled way means that the energy can be harnessed for all of the body's activities including . . . movement, digestion, repair of injured tissues, sensing the environment, and so on. Without enzymes, life is not possible.

---

1. I calculated this as follows: A 100-pound person weighs about 45 kg, of which 60 percent, or 27 kg, is water. Three hundred food calories would raise the temperature of 27 kg of water 11°C or about 19°F. Add this to the 98.6°F normal body temperature and you get 118°F.

RENNET CUSTARD

A STUDY OF ENZYME ACTION

One of the first steps in the digestion of milk is denaturing milk protein, or curdling it, so it becomes more solid. If milk remained a liquid, it would quickly pass through the stomach before it could be digested. But curdled milk moves slowly enough for digestion to take place.

Many things will denature milk protein, including heat and acids (look back at chapter 5 for more about this). In the stomachs of mammals, milk protein is denatured by an enzyme called *rennin* (or, commercially, *rennet*).

Rennet used to be prepared commercially from the linings of calves' stomachs. But today you can buy vegetable-based rennet tablets in some health food stores or on the internet. Rennet is used for preparing cottage cheese and thickening milk desserts. The next experiment will show you some of the properties of enzymes by varying the conditions necessary for the enzyme to work.

MATERIALS & EQUIPMENT

- 3 teaspoons water
- vegetable-based liquid rennet
- 1½ cups whole milk

- 6 teaspoons sugar

- vanilla extract

- measuring cups and spoons

- 3 (6-ounce) clear custard cups

- masking tape

- a pen or marker

- a spoon

- a saucepan

- a candy thermometer

PROCEDURE

1   Put 1 teaspoon of the water in each of the three cups. Add a drop of rennet to each and swirl to mix. Label each cup, using masking tape. They should read "cold," "110°F," and "160°F."

2   Put ½ cup of the cold milk in a measuring cup. Add 2 teaspoons of the sugar and a dash (less than ¼ teaspoon) of vanilla extract and stir well. Pour the mixture into the cup labeled "cold" and stir well.

3   Mix another ½ cup of the milk with sugar and vanilla. Warm this in a saucepan until its temperature is 110°F (43°C). Pour the mixture into the cup labeled "110°F" and stir well.

4   Make another milk mixture and heat this one to 160°F (71°C). Pour it into the cup labeled "160°F" and stir well. Let the mixtures stand, without disturbing them, until they set (if they do).

OBSERVATIONS

In which cup does the custard become firm most quickly? In which does it fail to set? How does this support the idea that enzymes are proteins? (Hint: What happens to proteins when they are heated to a high temperature?) What does this tell you about the amount of an enzyme needed to cause a reaction? Try the experiment with two drops of rennet and see if it makes a difference.

Do an experiment to see if rennet will work on other proteins. Substitute soybean milk, skim milk, almond milk, nonfat dry milk, or evaporated milk. Suppose you denature the milk some other way, like boiling it. Let the boiled milk cool to 110°F (43°C) before adding it to the rennet. How do your findings support the idea that rennin, like many other enzymes, controls only one reaction—in this case, denaturing milk protein?

CUT APPLES

KIWI STOPS THE BROWNING

The browning-of-fruit reaction studied in Vitamin C Fruit Salad (see chapter 6, pages 121–24) is more complicated than simple oxidation. An enzyme called *polyphenol oxidase* is involved. This enzyme causes certain compounds in cells to react with oxygen and become brown or gray. The reaction is similar to human skin turning brown in the sun. When the cells are intact, the enzyme and the compounds in the tissues (the phenols) are not in contact. When you cut an apple, the enzyme is released to act on the phenols and the browning reaction starts.

Is there any way to stop or slow down enzymatic browning? Do the next experiment and find out.

MATERIALS & EQUIPMENT

- a kiwifruit
- an apple
- a paring knife
- a new sponge
- scissors

PROCEDURE

1   Peel the brown skin off the kiwi with the paring knife and slice the fruit.

2   Cut out a piece of the sponge about the same size as a slice of kiwi.

3   Cut the apple in half. Place a slice of kiwi on the cut surface of one half of the apple. Place the piece of sponge on the cut surface of the other half of the apple.

4 Wait at least 1 hour, or until the exposed surface of the apple is brown. Lift the sponge and the piece of kiwi.

OBSERVATIONS

What color is the apple under the kiwi and under the sponge? The sponge was the control to see what happens when the surface is shielded from the air. Is shielding from air sufficient to slow down the browning reaction? There obviously is some substance in the kiwi that interferes with the browning reaction. In lemons that substance is vitamin C, also called ascorbic acid. Kiwis are another source of this compound. You might want to compare how kiwis, lemons, and a solution of vitamin C slow down enzymatic browning in apples. Design an experiment to do this.

JELL-O WITH PINEAPPLE
HOW HEAT AFFECTS AN ENZYME

If you read the instructions on a box of Jell-O, you are warned never to add fresh or frozen pineapple to the dessert. This warning is a perfect opening for a science experiment. Fresh pineapple contains an enzyme called *bromelain* that breaks down proteins. Gelatin desserts are protein and the bromelain in fresh pineapple would break down the protein so the dessert wouldn't gel. Since the enzymes themselves are also protein, it makes sense that heat can denature the enzyme so that it becomes inactive. Do the next experiment to see the effect of heat on enzyme action.

MATERIALS & EQUIPMENT

- a ripe, fresh pineapple
- water
- a package of Jell-O
- a large sharp knife
- 6 clear plastic cups
- a marker
- a plate
- a small saucepan
- a bowl
- measuring cups and spoons

PROCEDURE

1   Since pineapples are difficult to cut, get an adult to help you. Cut the pineapple into quarters. Taking one quarter, cut away the rind and the hard inner core. Then cut the fruit into bite-size pieces. Make them all the same size.

2   You are going to heat the pieces of pineapple for different lengths of time in the microwave. Raw pineapple will be the control. Mark one of the plastic cups "raw" and put 2 pieces of fresh pineapple into that cup. Mark

the rest of the cups as follows: "10 seconds," "30 seconds," "1 minute," "2 minutes," and "boiled."

3   Put 8 pieces of pineapple on a plate in a microwave oven. Microwave on high for 10 seconds. Quickly remove 2 pieces and put them in the cup marked "10 seconds." Immediately microwave the remaining pineapple on high for 20 seconds. Remove 2 pieces and put them in the cup marked "30 seconds." Microwave the remaining pineapple for 30 seconds and then remove 2 pieces and put them in the cup marked "1 minute." Microwave the last 2 pieces for another minute. Remove them and put them in the cup marked "2 minutes."

4   Next, put 2 pieces of pineapple in a small saucepan. Cover with water and boil them for 5 minutes. Drain off the water and place these pieces in the last cup marked "boiled."

5   Mix the Jell-O according to the directions on the package. Spoon 4 tablespoons of liquid Jell-O into each cup, and then put them in the refrigerator to cool.

OBSERVATIONS

Which cups gelled? Do your findings support the idea that a high temperature alone is not enough to "kill" an enzyme? Is the length of time the enzyme is exposed to a high heat also a factor?

Other fruits also contain protein-splitting enzymes. Design an experiment using Jell-O to see which fruits they are. The next experiment will give you a hint.

BAKED STEAK

ACIDS, BASES, AND ENZYME ACTION

This is a very ambitious experiment. It is also my favorite. The scientists at *Scientific American* magazine thought it was very clever. Who doesn't like high praise!

Papain is an enzyme that is commercially prepared from papayas, a tropical fruit. It is one of a number of enzymes found in plants and animals that break down proteins. For this reason, papain is sold as a meat tenderizer.

The purpose of this experiment is to answer two questions:

- Is meat treated with papain more tender than untreated meat?

- Does an acid or a base have an effect on the tenderizing activity of papain?

Of course, to answer these questions we have to have a way of measuring meat tenderness. Here's where science gets creative. I tried cutting the meat with a knife and piercing it with a fork and estimating the force I exerted. But this kind of measurement is very subjective and inaccurate. So I finally came up with the idea of feeding my experiment to an unsuspecting friend, one piece of meat at a time, and counting the number of chews before swallowing; the more tender the meat, the fewer the chews.

Needless to say, counting chews is not the most precise method of measuring tenderness. Two pieces of meat, prepared in exactly the same manner, might require different numbers of chews depending on quite a few variables. These include: the sizes of the pieces, whether or not there was gristle, how it tasted, how dry the chewer's mouth was, whether or not the chewer expected it to be tender, and how hungry the chewer was.

Since there are so many known possibilities of error, the procedure for this experiment is the most elaborate one in this book. You will be taking precautions wherever possible to reduce the sources of error and you will be using statistics on your data. Statistics is a branch of math that uses different mathematical operations on data to reveal results that might be obscured by a lot of variability.

MATERIALS & EQUIPMENT

- ¾ pound round steak (When you buy the steak, look for the most evenly red piece with very little fat and gristle and a uniform thickness.)
- water
- ¾ teaspoon unseasoned meat tenderizer
- vinegar
- baking soda
- a sharp knife
- a cutting board
- 6 small bowls
- index cards
- a pencil and paper
- 5 juice glasses
- measuring spoons
- 5 spoons
- scissors
- a broiling pan
- 6 plates
- a pot with a cover
- a fork
- a barrier for the table or a blindfold
- a hungry friend who doesn't know anything about your experiment (Tell your friend you will call when you are ready.)

PROCEDURE

1   Trim any fat and gristle from the meat and cut the trimmed meat into ¾-inch cubes. Try to keep the size of the cubes as uniform as possible. Pierce each piece of meat twice with a fork. (This is to allow the solutions you will be putting on the meat to penetrate inside.) Mix up all the cubes of meat in a pile.

2   Set the six small bowls in a row. Deal out the cubes of meat, as you would deal cards, into the bowls to form six equal groups of meat cubes. Try to get the same number in each group. If you have any extra pieces, put them in the last (control) group. Set a folded index card behind each bowl and number them 1 to 6.

3   Put juice glasses in front of groups 1 to 5 and put 2 tablespoons of water in each glass. Put 2 tablespoons of water on the meat in group 6.

4   Put ¼ teaspoon of the meat tenderizer in the glasses in front of groups 1, 2, and 3.

5   Put ½ teaspoon of the vinegar in the solutions for groups 2 and 4.

6   Put ½ teaspoon of the baking soda in the glasses for groups 3 and 5.

7   So, the solutions you've created for each group are:

      Group 1: meat tenderizer and water

      Group 2: meat tenderizer, acid, water

      Group 3: meat tenderizer, base, water

      Group 4: acid, water

Group 5: base, water

Group 6: water

Stir each solution with a different spoon and pour it over its group of meat cubes. Be sure to thoroughly moisten all sides of all the cubes of meat in each group.

1

¼ TEASPOON MEAT TENDERIZER
2 TABLESPOONS WATER

2

¼ TEASPOON MEAT TENDERIZER
½ TEASPOON VINEGAR
2 TABLESPOONS WATER

3

¼ TEASPOON MEAT TENDERIZER
½ TEASPOON BAKING SODA
2 TABLESPOONS WATER

4

½ TEASPOON VINEGAR
2 TABLESPOONS WATER

5

½ TEASPOON BAKING SODA
2 TABLESPOONS WATER

6

2 TABLESPOONS WATER

8 Preheat the oven to 400°F (204°C). Let the meat stand in the solutions while the oven is preheating and you complete the next step.

9 The order in which each piece of meat is chewed can affect your results. The best way to reduce this source of error is to present the pieces of meat in a completely random order. Here's one way to come up with a random list of numbers:

A. Cut index cards into as many small squares as the total number of pieces of meat in your experiment. If you have 6 groups of 10 pieces each, you will need 60 small squares.

B. Put the numeral "1" on as many squares of card as you have pieces of meat in Group 1. If you have 10 pieces, 10 squares of index card should be marked "1." Do the same for groups 2, 3, 4, 5, and 6.

C. Put all the numbered squares in a large pot. Put the lid on it and shake it to mix up all the squares. Draw out one square at a time, without looking, and mark down the number on a piece of paper. The order might look something like this: 4, 4, 6, 6, 6, 2, 1, 1, 3, 5, 6, 4, etc.

10 After you have made out your table of random numbers, drain the solutions from each bowl and put the drained meat on the broiling pan in separate groups. Keep the groups in the right order so you know which is which. Arrange the meat in a single layer with the pieces spaced fairly evenly so all the pieces will be heated the same amount. Bake for 15 minutes.

11 While the meat is baking, prepare a sheet of paper to record your data. There is one provided for you on page 204.

Test the meat for doneness by pressing with a fork. It should be springy and firm. Meat that is rare will be softer, as all the protein has not been set by heat.

DATA FOR NUMBER OF CHEWS

GROUP	1	2	3	4	5	6

AVERAGES

12 Put each group of cubes on a separate plate and label each plate using your numbered index cards again. Set up a table with some kind of barrier so your friend cannot see where each piece comes from, or blindfold your friend.

13 Show your friend where to sit. Say: "I'm going to give you pieces of baked steak to eat. I am testing the meat for tenderness. Please count the number of chews you need for each piece before you swallow it. Chew as naturally as possible."

14 Your table of random numbers tells you the order of choosing pieces of meat. If the first three numbers were 4, 4, 6, you would give your friend a piece from Group 4, and another piece from Group 4 and a piece from Group 6, in that order. Check off each number on your table as your friend chews the meat.

15 Record the number of chews for each piece in the proper column on your data sheet. When you have the data for all the pieces of meat, take the average for each group.

OBSERVATIONS

Was the meat treated with tenderizer more tender than untreated meat? (Compare the averages for Group 1 and Group 6.) Did acid or base alone affect meat tenderness? (Compare Groups 4 and 5 with Group 6.) Did acid have an effect on the action of the enzyme? (Compare Groups 1 and 2.) Did a base have an effect on enzyme action? (Compare Groups 1 and 3.)

The knowledge we get in science is a collaboration of many scientists, who repeat one another's experiments. After an experiment is repeated over and over again, the truth is evident to everyone. I did this experiment and I'm happy to share my results with you a little later. My experiment is considered a pilot—an experiment to see if the procedure works well enough to produce interesting results. Your numbers may be different but you will probably come to the same conclusions.

You can use the procedure for this experiment to test many other substances. See if you get similar results with another acid, such as vitamin C. Try the experiment on other kinds of meat. Find out if the enzyme has any other effect on meat, like juiciness. Can you think of a way to modify the procedure so that you can measure juiciness? You might find that using another kind of meat, like hamburger, is useful for studying the enzyme's effect on juiciness. You might also do an experiment to see if you can denature the enzyme by heating it. Boil an enzyme solution before you put it on the meat and compare its activity with an unheated enzyme in solution.

DATA FOR NUMBER OF CHEWS

GROUP	1	2	3	4	5	6
	26	42	25	54	44	45
	35	33	28	53	22	29
	29	25	20	48	27	54
	32	35	18	30	47	37
						60
AVERAGES	30.5	33.75	22.75	46.25	35.0	45.0

THE RIPENING HORMONE

As bananas ripen, the green pigment in the skin, called chlorophyll, is broken down chemically and disappears. The yellow pigments, called *carotenes* and *flavones*, which have been here all the time, are revealed once the chlorophyll disappears. Chemical changes occur in the flesh of the fruit as well: starch changes to sugar; pectin (a carbohydrate found in unripe fruit) breaks down, losing its stiffness; and the flesh softens.

MATERIALS & EQUIPMENT

- 7 very green bananas

- 1 very ripe banana

- a plastic bag and twist fastener

- 2 small brown paper bags (lunch-size bags work well)

- plastic wrap

PROCEDURE

Set up the bananas in their environments as follows:

1 Put two green bananas in a paper bag and fold the top over several times to seal out the air.

2 Put one green banana and the very ripe banana in the other paper bag and fold over the top.

3 Put two green bananas in a plastic bag. Twist the top and fasten with a twist fastener.

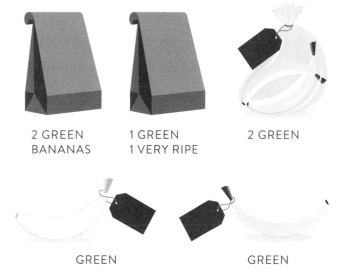

2 GREEN BANANAS

1 GREEN 1 VERY RIPE

2 GREEN

GREEN

GREEN

4 Wrap one green banana in several layers of plastic wrap. Make sure it is sealed tightly at each end.

5 Leave one green banana exposed to the air.

6 Leave the fruit alone for 4 or 5 days to ripen. Do not open any of the bags during this period. Then examine all the fruit. Which fruit is still green? Which is most yellow? Which has the most brown? You can eat the ripe bananas or put them back and allow the experiment to continue for another day or so.

OBSERVATIONS

Which banana ripened most quickly? Which banana turned brown fastest? Did the ripe banana have an effect on the rate at which the unripe banana ripened? What evidence is there that ripening fruit somehow changes the environment?

Ripening fruit "breathes," or *respires*. This means that it takes up oxygen and gives off carbon dioxide. Oxygen is essential for the chemical reactions involved in ripening. In addition, ripening fruit gives off another gas, called *ethylene*. Not only is ethylene a product of ripening fruit; in some mysterious way it also stimulates the further ripening of the fruit. For this reason it has been called the "ripening hormone." (Hormones are chemicals produced by living things that stimulate cellular changes.)

Paper bags tend to keep the ethylene in, but they are porous enough to allow oxygen (and ethylene) to pass through. Plastic bags do not allow the free flow of oxygen or ethylene. In this experiment, the green banana in the paper bag with the ripe banana should ripen most quickly. (Can you state why?) The green bananas in the paper bag should ripen faster than the bananas in the plastic bag. The banana left exposed to air has an unlimited supply of oxygen, so it will turn brown most quickly. You will notice that the side of this banana that rests on the counter will ripen more quickly than the other sides, because it has the most intimate contact with its own ethylene. The banana that is tightly wrapped in plastic has no oxygen supply and should ripen most slowly. (However, if all the air is not sealed out of the package, this banana will ripen first—can you see why?) Now can you see why bananas are sealed in plastic in many supermarkets?

FOR FURTHER STUDY

The green mold that grows on citrus fruits (for instance, lemons and oranges) gives off so much ethylene that a single moldy lemon has been known to greatly speed up the ripening of five hundred green lemons. If you should come across a moldy lemon, you might want to test its effect on unripe fruit. Put it in a paper bag along with an unripe pear, plum, peach, or avocado.

You have probably heard the old cliché, "A rotten apple spoils the whole barrel." Do your results show how this saying originated?

SCIENCE EXPERIMENTS WE DO EAT

Prehistoric human beings obtained food by hunting for meat and gathering edible plants and nuts. And they spent most of their time doing it. Food preservation was a problem. With the exception of nuts, unprocessed, fresh food would soon be feeding insect larvae, worms, mold, and bacteria, making it unfit at worst or unappetizing at best for human consumption. Our distaste for spoiled food is nature's way of protecting us from eating it and getting sick. Through trial and error and through science we've gradually learned how to preserve food so that it can be stored for later use.

When you walk the aisles in a supermarket, the shelves are lined with the results of many science experiments. We now understand basic principles of food preservation so that most canned goods can last five years and dry packaged goods can last ten to twelve years. The perimeter of the supermarket is where you'll find the fresh produce, dairy, meats, and deli. They are the more perishable products. All supermarkets have this same basic floor plan.

But preserving food is now only part of what the huge processed-food industry does. It also produces an incredible variety of packaged dinners, cereals, snacks, drinks, desserts, and treats that have been engineered to appeal to our senses to the point that we crave them and can't eat just a little bit. Food manufacturers use a range of additives that bleach, stabilize, tenderize, thicken, harden, clarify, fortify, keep dry, keep moist, keep crisp, keep firm, or improve the appearance of their products. Such additives can make food more convenient or nutritious, give it a longer shelf life, and make it more attractive to the consumer, thus increasing the sales and profits of the manufacturers. But we are now taking a second look at many of these prepackaged products. Perhaps some of these foods are causing the obesity epidemic in America. In many cases, science has been used to get you "hooked" on a food so you overconsume it and neglect to eat a healthy diet. Yes, too much junk food in childhood can lead to medical problems in later life.

In this chapter I'll discuss how science has both helped and harmed us through processed foods. First, the science behind food preservation.

BEEF JERKY

DRYING AND CURING

One way of slowing down or stopping the growth of bacteria and mold is to remove moisture, since moisture is essential for the growth of most microorganisms. When Native Americans hung strips of buffalo meat in the sun and wind, they didn't know they were creating a less desirable environment for bacteria. But they did know that dried meat (which came to be called "jerky" after the Spanish word for this food, *charqui*) remained edible a lot longer than fresh meat. Also, it weighed less, making it easier to carry when they traveled over the range.

You could compare the rate of spoilage by leaving a piece of fresh beef and a piece of commercially prepared beef jerky at room temperature to see which spoils first. However, the results are quite predictable and completely inedible. Here are a couple of more appetizing scientific questions: Is it better to dry beef in the air or in the oven? Does salt have an effect on the drying process? Experiment and find out!

MATERIALS & EQUIPMENT

- 1-pound flank steak

- a cutting board

- salt (coarse or kosher, if possible)

- a roasting pan with rack (a cake rack, or use the rack in the oven)

- string or a long skewer

- a sharp knife

- a heavy bottle or mallet

- a food or postal scale

- paper and a pencil

PROCEDURE

1 Trim all the fat from the steak. Cutting with the grain of the meat, make strips that are about 1 inch wide and ¼ inch thick. Since the steak is probably more than ¼ inch thick, you will have to split the steak through the thicker middle area by inserting the knife between the layers of muscle and cutting lengthwise. Ask an adult to help with the slicing. There should be eight to ten strips.

2 Lay the strips out on the cutting board and pound them with a heavy bottle (like a glass ketchup bottle) or a mallet until they are very thin. Divide the strips into two groups. Try to keep the two groups about equal to each other in the size and weight of strips. Sprinkle salt heavily on one group of strips. Pound the salt in. Turn the strips over and pound salt into the other side.

3 Divide the strips into four groups that will receive different treatment:
Group 1: oven-dried, salted
Group 2: oven-dried, unsalted
Group 3: air-dried, salted
Group 4: air-dried, unsalted

4 Weigh each strip carefully on a food or postal scale. Record its weight. Note its position on the drying rack, if it is to be oven-dried, or its position on a string or skewer for air-drying.

5 You can hang strips for air-drying over a piece of string strung between two chairs. (I hung my strips by sticking a long shish kebab skewer through one end. The ends of the skewer were rested on the backs of two chairs, suspending the strips between them.) Hanging them near a radiator will shorten the drying time.

6 Place the pan with the strips to be oven-dried in a *very* low oven. It should be set at the lowest possible setting, about 150°F (66°C). Leave the oven door slightly ajar.

7 When dry, the jerky will be shriveled and dark. My oven-dried beef jerky took 8½ hours to dry. The air-dried strips took about 36 hours.

OBSERVATIONS

The strips will feel lighter in weight when dry. Weigh each strip and calculate the percentage of weight loss using the following formula:

$$Percentage\ of\ weight\ loss = \frac{fresh\ weight - dried\ weight}{fresh\ weight} \times 100$$

After the oven-dried jerky cools, try breaking it. Try breaking an air-dried strip. Which treatment gives the crispiest jerky? Which gives the toughest? Does salt have an effect on the drying process? Eating the jerky will give you some of the answers.

FOR FURTHER STUDY

Pounding salt (or other spices) into meat is called dry-curing. Salt draws moisture out of meat; the water in the muscle cells flows out to the saltier area outside the cells.

Try making beef jerky with a wet-curing or brine treatment. Soak the meat strips overnight in a mixture of ½ cup coarse salt in 2 cups water. Pat dry with a paper towel and use the air-drying or oven-drying procedure. Be sure to air- or oven-dry untreated strips simultaneously so you can compare results. Which is more effective, dry-curing or brine-curing, for the drying process?

ZUCCHINI

FREEZING AND THAWING

Lower the temperature and you slow down the growth rate of microorganisms. That's the principle of refrigeration. But, as you undoubtedly know, food can and does spoil even under refrigeration if you keep it long enough. Freezing, however, stops microorganisms from growing. It doesn't kill them, so if thawing occurs, the microbes will start growing again. (That's why thawed food should be cooked and eaten as soon as possible.)

The main advantage of freezing is that it changes food from its fresh state less than any other method of food preservation. Even so, freezing can change the texture of foods, especially vegetables. This doesn't matter much if the vegetable is to be cooked, which would change its texture anyhow. But freezing vegetables like lettuce or tomatoes that are to be used raw in salads will give disappointing results. (Don't take my word for this—freeze and thaw some lettuce and see for yourself.)

Frozen-food companies have spent a great deal of time and money developing ways to keep frozen vegetables as much like fresh as possible. In the next experiment you will investigate the difference between your home-freezing technique and that of commercial frozen-food producers.

MATERIALS & EQUIPMENT

- 1 package commercially frozen zucchini
- 1 small young zucchini squash
- paper towels
- a knife
- 2 plastic sandwich bags with twist fasteners
- a freezer thermometer (optional)

PROCEDURE

1   Put a package of commercially frozen zucchini into your freezer. Wash and pat dry the fresh zucchini squash. Slice into ½-inch slices. Put half of the slices into a plastic sandwich bag. Close tightly with a twist fastener. Put the bag into the freezer.

2   Put the other half of the sliced zucchini into another plastic bag, fasten, and refrigerate. This is your control group, against which the effects of freezing will be compared. (The best experiments are "controlled" experiments—ones in which changes are introduced systematically, so that differences can be linked to the changes you make in the setup.)

3   The next day, take out the home-frozen zucchini and the package of commercially frozen zucchini. Allow them to thaw completely. This may take several hours. Compare the texture of the home-frozen squash with that of the commercially frozen and the unfrozen.

OBSERVATIONS

Which zucchini is firmest? Which is softest?

Frozen water has more volume (is less dense) than an equal weight of liquid water. If you've ever seen an aluminum can of soda stretched out of shape because it was left in the freezer to cool down quickly and then forgotten, you know what I mean. Put a stalk of celery in the freezer and let it freeze overnight. Defrost it and see the difference. Plant cells contain a great deal of water. When this water expands as it turns to ice, it damages the cell walls, so the vegetable loses its crispness.

Commercially frozen zucchini is flash-frozen at about –20°F. How cold is your freezer? (You can measure with a freezer thermometer if you want.) When the freezing process is slow, larger ice crystals form. Which zucchini must have had the largest ice crystals?

Put all the zucchini—including the refrigerated control—into a saucepan with about a cup of water. Bring to a boil and simmer for about 5 minutes. Drain and season with butter, salt, and pepper. Can you still tell the difference between fresh-cooked zucchini, home-frozen, and commercially frozen?

FOR FURTHER STUDY

Check out the effect of freezing on meat. Cut a piece of raw steak in half and freeze one half. Refrigerate the other half. A day or so later, defrost the frozen steak. Compare it in appearance to the unfrozen half. Broil both and taste to see if there is a difference.

A food chemist at a meat-packing plant told me that animal cells are somewhat affected by ice crystals. The cells are enclosed in flexible protein membranes that can be broken down by sharp ice crystals, making the meat somewhat more tender. He also said that the difference was so slight he didn't think the average person would be able to detect it. Food chemists use a special instrument to measure the texture of meat.

In the Baked Steak experiment on page 199, I developed a highly sophisticated procedure for measuring the tenderness of meat by counting the average number of chews before swallowing. It may be sensitive enough to detect a difference here.

In researching for this revision, I came across a scientist in Sweden, Frederico Gomez, whose team is working on a technique to freeze a salad. There is a YouTube video that shows what they're doing. It seems that many of the plants that survive very cold winters have a certain sugar in their cells, called *trehalose*, which protects them from ice crystals. Dr. Gomez uses a vacuum and pulses from an electric field to get trehalose into the cells of parsnip slices and spinach leaves. I purchased some trehalose online and tried to get trehalose into the plants by soaking them in a 20 percent trehalose solution. I didn't have the vacuum or the electric field. No luck. But if you're looking for an ambitious science fair project, you just might want to tackle this.

CANNED FRUITS AND VEGETABLES

HIGH-ACID VS. LOW-ACID FOODS

Canned food was invented in 1809 when Napoleon Bonaparte held a contest to find a way to preserve food for his armies. The first "canned" goods were put in jars that were vacuum-sealed and then heated, killing all the microorganisms inside. (Of course, no one knew that this was what was happening. Louis Pasteur discovered microorganisms as the culprits in the spoilage of food and wine more than forty years later.) It has been said that if the canning process could have been kept a French national secret, Napoleon would have conquered the world. But by 1810, not only was the secret out, an Englishman had improved the process, using "tins"—steel cans lined with tin—instead of heavier jars.

Commercial canning today is one of the safest and longest-lasting ways of preserving food. Modern commercial canneries seal food in cans and pressure-cook them at about 250°F. (Pressure cookers are strong closed pots built to trap steam, which can be heated well above the boiling point of water, which is 212°F or 100°C. As a result, food cooks more quickly.) So canned food is not only sterile, it is also cooked. Home canning is a project you might want to do with the cook in your house. However, the equipment needed, and the temperatures and pressures involved, make it too difficult and elaborate a procedure for this book. So we will restrict our experimenting to commercially canned food.

One of the factors that determines the temperature needed to kill bacteria is the amount of acid in food. Bacteria do not grow as well in high-acid foods (those with a sour taste), like grapefruit, as they do in low-acid foods, like green beans. In fact, one of the dangers in home canning of green beans and other low-acid foods is that incomplete sterilization will allow deadly botulinum bacteria to grow.

These bacteria produce a substance that causes botulism, the most dreaded of all food poisoning. The poison causing botulism is so potent that the amount found in a single bean can kill an adult. The symptoms—vomiting, double vision, thirst, inability to swallow, thick saliva—appear within twenty-four hours after the affected food is eaten. Most cases (60 to 70 percent) are fatal, and recovery can take up to six months in those that are not. The reason botulism is such a danger in low-acid home canning is that the spores (the reproductive "seeds") of the bacteria are very common in gardens, and they can be very resistant to heat. The low-acid foods they are likely to grow in must be kept at boiling temperature for at least 20 minutes in order to kill them. Acidic foods, like most varieties of tomatoes, do not provide such a hospitable environment, so botulinum bacteria rarely grow in high-acid canned goods.

Measuring acidity is one of the most common jobs of chemists. It is fun, and it can have surprising results. Taste alone will not always tell you which food has more or less acid than another. In this experiment you'll measure canned fruits and vegetables for acidity.

MATERIALS & EQUIPMENT

- a selection of the smallest cans of a few of the following: carrots, green beans, cherries, pineapple, apricots, peaches, pears, tomatoes, beets, asparagus, peas, corn, lima beans (look for the brands with the fewest added ingredients)

- measuring spoons

- red cabbage indicator (see page 20)

- a pencil and paper

- small juice glasses

- teaspoons

PROCEDURE

Most foods are on the acid side. Some are more acidic than others. The method used to rank them is called *titration*. You will be counting the number of teaspoons of fruit or vegetable juice it takes to produce the color change that shows the presence of acid.

1 For each canned item you are going to test, you'll need a small juice glass and a teaspoon for stirring. Put 2 tablespoons of red cabbage indicator in each glass.

2 Add juice from the first canned food, 1 teaspoon at a time. Stir each time you add juice. Keep a record of the number of teaspoons you need to get the color to change to acid pink. Then move on to titrate the next food you are going to test.

OBSERVATIONS

Rank your fruits and vegetables according to acidity. Check your results with the table here.

You may get results that differ from this ranking. Differences can be caused by the presence of flavorings and other juices added during the canning process. Check labels to see if you are using the most simply processed product with the fewest additives.

MOST ACID
Cherries
Pineapple
Peaches
Apricots
Pears
Tomatoes
Carrots
Green beans
Beets
Asparagus
Lima beans
Corn
LEAST ACID

CHOCOLATE PUDDING

CARRAGEENAN STABILIZATION

Ever see a watery liquid seep out of a pudding? If not, it's because of *carrageenan*, a carbohydrate extracted from sun-dried Irish moss seaweed. Cooks in Ireland and France began using it hundreds of years ago as an ingredient in milk puddings. Carrageenan is the most effective stabilizer for milk-based foods because of the unique way in which its molecules combine with milk protein.

In this experiment you'll see the effect of carrageenan in chocolate pudding. Since all pudding mixes contain carrageenan, you'll need to make pudding from scratch in order to observe the effect.

MATERIALS & EQUIPMENT

- baker's (unsweetened) chocolate
- 1 cup sugar
- salt
- a double boiler
- 2 medium bowls
- 16 ounces evaporated milk (check the label to make sure it contains carrageenan)
- measuring cup and spoons
- spoons
- 2 cups fresh milk
- 6 tablespoons cornstarch
- 2 teaspoons vanilla extract
- a knife for making level measure

PROCEDURE

1   Put 1 ounce (a square) of chocolate in the top of a double boiler over boiling water and heat until melted.

2   Slowly stir in ½ cup sugar, 1¾ cups of the evaporated milk with carrageenan, and a dash of salt.

3   While this mixture is heating, dissolve 3 level tablespoons of cornstarch in ¼ cup of the evaporated milk. Slowly add this mixture to the hot milk mixture, stirring constantly.

4   Continue heating and stirring the pudding until it is thickened and doesn't taste of raw cornstarch, about 10 minutes.

5   Remove the pudding from the heat. When it is slightly cool, stir in 1 teaspoon of vanilla extract. Pour the mixture into a bowl. Allow the pudding to cool to room temperature before refrigerating.

6   Repeat the recipe, substituting fresh milk for evaporated. This pudding, your control, will not have carrageenan in it.

OBSERVATIONS

Which pudding forms a skin? Allow the puddings to remain in the refrigerator for at least a day before eating. As they age, which one "weeps" more (develops more watery fluid around the edges)? How would you describe the stabilizing effects of carrageenan?

Carrageenan combines with milk protein in a way that prevents butterfat from separating from the watery part of milk. For this reason, puddings that contain carrageenan should not "weep," while those made without carrageenan weep as they age. The skin that forms on the control pudding is coagulated milk protein. Since carrageenan binds this protein, keeping the pudding smooth, skin doesn't form on the experimental pudding.

Carrageenan is also used to add "body" to soft drinks, to prevent large ice crystals from forming in ice cream, and to prevent the oil from separating in whipped topping and the butterfat from separating in evaporated milk. Why does the pudding made with evaporated milk taste distinctively different from that made with fresh milk? It is one example of the many food additives.

Food additives are presently at the center of an ongoing storm of controversy. Food manufacturers have been known to use additives that have not been proved safe; further, some substances in common use have been proved unsafe, or potentially unsafe, and have been taken off the market. Many people feel there is a risk involved in eating food to which anything has been added. This extends to farming where organic food growers emphasize that they do not use chemical fertilizers or pesticides.

For people with allergies or other special sensitivities, eating foods with additives may truly pose a risk. But food additives are regulated by the Food and Drug Administration of the federal government, and new additives are subjected to extensive testing before they can be placed on the market. The FDA has compiled a list of additives that are Generally Regarded as Safe (the GRAS List, which can be found on the FDA's website). For most people, the chances of developing serious side effects from the long-term use of currently approved food additives are very slim.

MEASURING CALORIES

Food is the fuel that gives you the energy to be alive—to grow, move, sense the world, and heal from illness and injury. This energy comes from the chemical reaction between fuel and oxygen. If you burn fuel in air, this energy is released quickly in the form of the heat and light from the flame. In your body, however, this energy release is controlled by enzymes so that it can be used for all the life processes, and the heat that is released is relatively low, not high enough to burn you up. It's simple to burn a piece of fuel and measure the heat energy released by seeing how it changes the temperature of a measured amount of water. All you need is a way to burn the fuel so that all the heat goes into heating up the water. I introduced the calorimeter on page 133.

Scientists all over the world use the metric system for all their measurements. Unfortunately, in daily life in the United States we use the imperial system, so you have to do some math to convert. But I'm going to stick to the metric system to show how we measure calories—the unit of heat energy that tells us how much energy there is in every kind of food. A calorie is defined as the amount of heat needed to raise one gram of water (also 1 milliliter or one cubic centimeter, cc) one degree Celsius.

The instrument that measures calories, called a calorimeter, is found in every food science laboratory. The chamber where the food sample is incinerated is very well insulated, so no heat is lost to the atmosphere. Measuring calories is a quantitative activity. An improvised calorimeter using an empty soda can and an open flame is not the most accurate way of measuring the calories in foods but you will get results and you can calculate your percentage of error from accepted values for food. You will also get a feeling for how "bench" scientists (those who work in labs) do their jobs.

This is a fairly elaborate experiment that bears repeating a number of times, to check and double-check your results. You'll have to build some of your apparatus (something scientists have always done) and you'll need some inexpensive measuring instruments that I could find only on the web. But this procedure has a lot of potential for examining many foods and will give you an appreciation for the importance of accurate measurement in science.

MATERIALS & EQUIPMENT

To make the stand:

- 4 wire coat hangers

- strong twine

- needle-nose pliers for shaping

- a wire cutter (sometimes in the pliers)

To do the experiment:

- water

- Brazil nuts

- aluminum foil

- clean, empty aluminum soda can with pop tab still attached

- a measuring cup that measures milliliters

- a postage scale that weighs grams (it's helpful, but not necessary, if you can measure tenths of grams)

- a knife

- a Celsius lab thermometer (you can buy one online)

- a "church key" can opener

- a butane lighter

- paper towels

- a potholder

- marshmallows, Cheetos (optional)

PROCEDURE

1   A. Bend two wire coat hangers in half to form the four legs.

A.

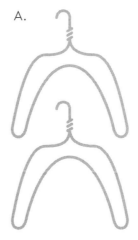

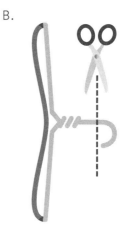

B.

B. Cut an inch or so off the end of the hooks. You only need about 3 inches of wire after the twisted part to make hooks.

C. Bend the curved hanger hooks (which do the hanging) toward each other at right angles to the legs that connect the two sides to form a bridge at the top of the stand.

D. Cut four 10-inch lengths of wire from the other two coat hangers. Note how the ends are crimped to hold the legs in place.

C.

E. Wrap twine around the top to reinforce that bond.

F. Make hooks out of the remaining wires as needed so you can adjust the height of the soda can over the flame.

D. and E.

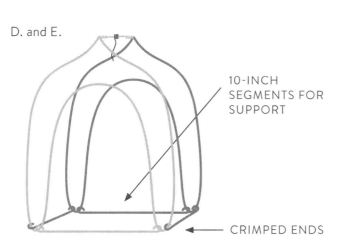

10-INCH SEGMENTS FOR SUPPORT

CRIMPED ENDS

F.

WIRE TO ADJUST HEIGHT OF CAN

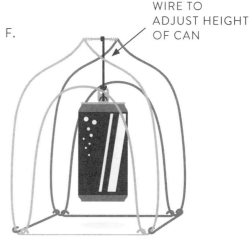

2   Make a data sheet as follows (I'm including data from one of my trials to give you an idea of what to expect):

FOOD	MASS OF FOOD in grams— initial	MASS OF FOOD in grams— final	INITIAL TEMP °C	FINAL TEMP °C	TEMP CHANGE Final— initial	MASS OF WATER in grams
Brazil Nut	3	0	29	70	41	200

3 Prepare for a trial: Spread a piece of foil on your countertop and put the stand on the foil. Pour 200 ml (cc) of water into an empty soda can. (You can use a measuring cup to measure milliliters or you can use the scale to measure grams. The beauty of the metric system is that one gram of water is one cubic centimeter—a cc—or one milliliter.) It's helpful if the starting temperature of the water is room temperature. That way you don't have to rush. With a knife, square off one of the ends of a Brazil nut. Weigh the nut. Stick the flat end of the nut on the point of the church key so that it is vertical. Measure and record the temperature of the water in the can. Remove the thermometer when you're done. Hang the can on the stand so that the bottom is about 2 inches above the top of the nut.

4 To do the trial, ask a grown-up to use a butane lighter to set fire to the bottom of the nut. It takes a few seconds to get the nut burning. As soon as the flame is established, move the nut under the soda can. Notice that when the flame touches the can, soot collects. This is pure carbon and an indication that the fuel is not burning completely. When fuel burns completely, carbon dioxide is produced, which is an invisible gas. However, if you move the can too far away from the flame, a lot of the heat is lost to the air. When the nut finally burns out, use a potholder to remove the can from the stand. Swirl it around to make sure the heated water is evenly distributed, since the water near the bottom of the can will be warmer than water near the surface. Take the temperature of the heated water. Weigh whatever is left of the burnt food.

NOW FOR THE MATH

Math is the "language" of science. It expresses the relationship between variables. Here we are looking at the relationship between the energy in a food and the change in temperature of water.

First: Calculate the change in temperature of the water:

Final temperature – Initial temperature = change in temperature

Second: Calculate how many calories were produced in 200 grams of water.

A calorie equals the amount of heat needed to raise one gram of water one degree Celsius. I raised 200 grams of water 41°C. So:

200g x 41°C = 8,200 calories

Third: A food calorie is 1,000 calories; the unit is Calorie with a capital C.

$$C = c \neq 1000$$

$$C = \frac{8200}{1000} = 8.2\ c$$

Fourth: How many grams of food were burned?

Initial weight – final weight = weight burned. In this case 3 grams were burned.

If you divide the calories by the weight loss, you get the amount of calories per gram of nut:

$$8.2C/3 = 2.73 \ C/gram$$

You can compare your results using the data on the Nutrition Facts on the Brazil nut package.

According to the label a portion (28g) contains 200 Cal. To get the number of calories/gram:

$$C/gram = 200/28 = 7.14 \ C/gram$$

This is considerably higher than my measurement. My percentage of error can be calculated as follows:

$$Percentage \ error = \frac{2.73}{7.14} \ x \ 100 = 38\%$$

What can explain this large error? The soot on the can shows that a lot of the nut was not burned completely. My scale was not very accurate—it didn't measure fractions of grams—and heat was lost to the air from the open flame and from the metal soda can. You can see what a challenge it is to build a homemade precise measuring instrument, but these results do show the relative caloric values of a number of foods.

If you measure other foods and compare your results to the Brazil nuts you will see that there is a ranking of higher-calorie foods to lower ones. I tried roasting a marshmallow under the soda can by putting it on the end of a skewer. But it melted and fell off.

HOW TO READ A NUTRITION FACTS LABEL

The Nutrition Facts label appears on every packaged food and on some fresh foods as well. There is a *lot* of information about the food, including the number of calories in a portion. All of the information comes from food science laboratories where there are well-established procedures for measuring.

This information is data that anyone can get if they repeat the procedures, which are published and available to the scientific community. Scientists are always checking one another's work. It keeps them honest. Cheating or "fudging" data sooner or later gets exposed. What the data mean, however, is always up to interpretation. So if you know how to read the scientific data that are published, you are armed to do some original investigations of your own. Be forewarned. Some of the information I'm going to give you shows how food companies are trying to keep important truths from the public.

I'm going to use the label on a potato chip bag as an example of what to look for when reading a Nutrition Facts label.

The serving size is measured by weight in imperial units (ounces) and metric units (grams). Note how many chips are in a serving. Here's where manufacturers

Nutrition Facts

Serving Size 1 oz. (28g/About 15 chips)

Amount Per Serving

Calories 160	Calories from Fat 90

	% Daily Value*
Total Fat 10g	**16%**
Saturated Fat 1g	**5%**
Trans Fat 0g	
Polysaturated Fat 2.5g	
Monounsaturated Fat 5g	
Cholesterol 0mg	**0%**
Sodium 170mg	**7%**
Potassium 350mg	**10%**
Total Carbohydrate 150mg	**5%**
Dietary Fiber 1g	**5%**
Sugars less than 1g	
Protein 2g	

Vitamin A 0%	•	Vitamin C 10%
Calcium 0%	•	Iron 2%
Vitamin E 6%	•	Thiamin 4%
Niacin 6%	•	Vitamin B 0%
Magnesium 4%	•	Zinc 2%

*Percent Daily Values are based on a 2,000-calorie diet. Your daily values may be higher or lower depending on your calorie needs.

	Calories:	2,000	2,500
Total Fat	Less than	65g	80g
Sat Fat	Less than	20g	25g
Cholesterol	Less than	300mg	300mg
Sodium	Less than	2,400mg	2,400mg
Potassium		3,500mg	3,500mg
Total Carbohydrate		300g	375g
Dietary Fiber		25g	30g

Calories per gram

Fat 9 • Carbohydrate 4 • Protein 4

Ingredients: Potatoes, Vegetable Oil (Sunflower, Corn and/or Canola Oil) and Salt
No Preservatives.

want to confuse you. Most people don't pay attention to the serving size of 15 chips. They often eat the whole bag. The number of calories multiplied by the number of servings in a bag will give the eater a truer measure of how many calories have been consumed, which can be more than 1,000 in one sitting. (Can you believe you ate the whole thing?)

The next list is measured only in grams. Check out the daily value in percentage on the right. This number is based on an average diet of 2,000 calories a day. Again the unit is *one portion*—15 chips give you 16 percent of the total fat you should consume for a day. Saturated fat (fat that is solid at room temperature) should be limited because your body can turn it into cholesterol—a fatty material that lines arteries and is linked to heart disease. Sodium is found in salt. It is necessary for a lot of body function but too much can lead to high blood pressure, which can lead to a stroke.

Total carbohydrate includes both starch and sugar. Fiber, also known as "roughage," is needed for healthy digestion. It is food for the helpful bacteria in your intestines. But you're not going to get much from 15 potato chips. No sugar has been added to this product. The protein in potato chips comes from the potato itself.

There are some essential vitamins and minerals in the chips but not enough to fulfill your daily requirement. Notice the asterisk that indicates that the measure is the standard 2,000-calorie diet, which may or may not apply to you. But they conveniently give you the values.

Now, about the ingredients. They are listed in the order of largest proportion to smallest. Notice "Potatoes" are listed first. This is a good thing because you know what you're getting—real potatoes. Here's an example of a different food product: water, glucose, citric acid, sodium citrate, sodium phosphate, potassium citrate, natural and artificial flavors, ester, gum, and artificial color. Know what it is? It's not a concoction some fiend mixed up in a laboratory. It is a lemon-lime-flavored soft drink designed specifically to replace the body salts lost during prolonged periods of intense athletic exercise. So in our lemon-lime soft drink, glucose—a sugar—is second to water. Citric acid and sodium citrate are the distinctive substances that make lemons and limes taste like lemons and limes.

Do a study of cold cereals to see how much sugar is in a serving. I found that the sugars in popular brands of cold cereal ranged from 4 grams per portion to 12 grams. There is some pressure on the Food and Drug Administration to change the Nutrition Facts labeling from "sugars" to "added sugar." Cereal manufacturers do extensive studies on people, giving them foods with measured amounts of sugar and asking them to rank how much they like it. As a result they know exactly how much sugar to put into a product to meet most people's "bliss point." The bliss point makes the food "crave-able" so that people are not satisfied with anything less sweet. What do you think are the consequences of this kind of marketing? Overeating? Addiction to certain kinds of foods? Tooth decay? (Did you know that fossils of jawbones of ancient humans had no tooth decay?)

Also, check out the portion size in the labeling. There is pressure on food manufacturers to publish the total number of calories in a package, which is easily calculated by multiplying the number of calories in a portion by the number of portions in the package.

Good nutrition for health is not a mystery. It is a balanced amount of carbohydrates, fats, proteins, vitamins, and minerals found in fresh food cooked from scratch. This doesn't mean you can't eat processed food (after all, cooking is a form of processing). But you should not eat *only* processed food. If you take in more calories a day than you use up with your activities, the extra calories are stored as fat in your body. The more you know about science, the better you will understand how to stay healthy.

COOKING TERMS AND INSTRUCTIONS

basting: To moisten food while it cooks, so that the surface doesn't dry out and flavor is added, coat it with its own juices or a prepared marinade. A pastry brush is helpful, and there are basters that work like giant eye droppers, but you can also use a spoon.

beating egg whites: Start with egg whites that are at room temperature. It is best to use an electric mixer for beating egg whites. (If you don't have one, use a rotary eggbeater or a wire whisk. You might want to have a friend handy to help when your arm gets tired.) Beat the whites on low speed until they become foamy, then increase the speed gradually to high and beat until the whites become stiff. They should have a glossy surface and will stand in peaks when you lift the beater slowly from the bowl. Don't overbeat egg whites or they will start to dry out.

boiling: When a liquid boils, bubbles are constantly rising to the surface and breaking. Water boils at sea level at 212°F or 100°C. Solutions may boil at higher temperatures.

creaming: Creaming is to mix a shortening, like butter, with other ingredients, such as sugar, until they are well blended. It is easiest to cream butter with an electric mixer, and the mixture will be fluffier and lighter in color if you do. If you don't have an electric mixer, you can do it by hand with a large spoon (a wooden spoon works well) and a lot of muscle. Either way, you should start with softened butter. To cream by hand, press down on the butter with the back of the spoon, drawing the spoon toward you across the bottom of the bowl. Turn the bowl as you go and periodically scrape around the sides of the bowl to collect the ingredients in the middle again. Continue creaming until the mixture is thoroughly combined and smooth.

cutting in: Cutting in distributes solid fat in flour by using a pastry blender or two knives until flour-coated fat particles are the size you want. If you have a pastry blender, roll the blades along the bottom of the bowl, then lift it up, turn the bowl, and slice down again. You'll need to stop and scrape off the blender and bring all the ingredients into the center every few turns. If you're using two knives, take a knife in each hand. Start with your hands close together over the center of the bowl then move them apart, drawing the two blades across each other, scraping the bottom of the bowl as you go.

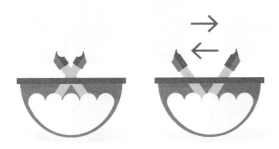

double boiler: Two pots where the upper, smaller one fits into the lower, larger one. The lower pot is filled with water. The purpose of a double boiler is to keep the temperature of ingredients in the upper pot at or slightly below the temperature of boiling water.

dropping by spoonfuls: Take a spoonful of batter for cookies or biscuits and push it off onto your baking sheet with another spoon or your fingers. Leave a couple of inches between drops to give them room to spread out as they bake.

folding: Folding is a way to combine delicate ingredients such as whipped cream or beaten egg whites with other foods without losing too much of the volume and the air bubbles. Add the whipped ingredient to the heavier ingredient and, using a rubber spatula, cut down into the mixture, slide across the bottom of the bowl, and bring some of the mixture up and over the surface of the other ingredients. Give the bowl a quarter turn and repeat this circular motion. Continue to fold just until the two ingredients are combined. If you fold too much, you'll lose more air than necessary, and your cake won't rise as high.

kneading dough: Flour your hands liberally, then dump the dough out onto a lightly floured surface and shape it into a ball. Pull the far end of the dough toward you, folding it over. Then, using the heels of your hands, push it away with a rolling motion. Give the dough a quarter turn and continue folding and pushing the dough, sprinkling flour on the dough as necessary to keep it from sticking. Get yourself into a rhythm and use your whole body, not just your arms, when you knead. You'll have to knead for about ten minutes to make the dough smooth and elastic.

measuring dry ingredients: Scoop up dry ingredients in your measuring cup, or spoon them lightly into the cup. Level off with a knife or other straight edge. Use this scoop-and-sweep method with your measuring spoons as well.

measuring liquids: Use a glass measuring cup with a spout for measuring liquids. Pour the liquid into the cup and check the measure at eye level. Liquids measured in measuring spoons should fill the spoon but not overflow.

preparing baking pans: For cakes, muffins, and cupcakes: Rub the inner surface of a baking dish with butter or vegetable fat. Then add a tablespoon or so of flour and swirl it

around in the pan to coat all the surfaces. Dump out any extra flour. For breads, cookies, or biscuits: Just grease the inside of the pan or the surface of the baking sheet. This should ensure that your cakes, breads, and cookies will not stick to the pan. You can also use nonstick cooking sprays with a butter flavor.

pressure cooker: A sturdy pot with an airtight top that can be sealed to contain food and water. When the pot is heated, the water changes to steam. The trapped steam can be heated to higher temperatures than boiling water, thus cooking food more quickly. All pressure cookers have a valve to slowly relieve the pressure so that the top can be removed safely.

separating eggs: Have two bowls ready, one for the white and one for the yolk. Gently crack the egg near its middle against the edge of a bowl, or by tapping it with a knife. Carefully pull apart the shell with your thumbs and fingertips. Tilt the egg so one half of the shell is above the other. The yolk will sink to the bottom half. Do this over one of the bowls. When you remove the top half of the shell the white will slip into the bowl. Pass the egg yolk from shell to shell until all the white has run into the bowl, then drop the egg yolk into a second bowl. Don't let any egg yolk mix with the whites. For egg whites to be beaten to the absolute peaks, they cannot be mixed with any fat. If you are separating several eggs, it is safer to let each white drop into a new bowl; that way if the yolk of one egg breaks, it won't ruin the whole bowl of whites.

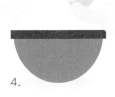

1.

2.

3.

4.   5.

simmering: A simmering liquid is below the boiling point. Bubbles form slowly and collapse just below the surface. Simmering is controlled by the amount of heat coming from the burner.

whipping cream: You can whip cream with an electric mixer, an eggbeater, or a wire whisk. Cream whips faster when cold, so if you are beating cream by hand, it might help to place the bowl of cream over a bowl of ice water. Beat the cream at high speed until soft peaks form when you raise the beater straight up. If you overbeat whipping cream, guess what? You'll get butter!

SCIENTIFIC GLOSSARY

acid: Any substance that can react with a base to form a salt. In water solutions an acid tastes sour, as in lemon juice or vinegar, but tasting is not a good method for testing for acids since many acids are dangerous. Sulfuric acid and nitric acid can burn the skin and eat away at metals. Common edible acids include citric acid in oranges and acetic acid in vinegar, which give foods a tart flavor, and ascorbic acid (vitamin C), needed by the body.

alchemist: A chemist who lived during the Middle Ages whose aim was to change other metals into gold. A lot of their procedures, discovered by trial and error, are still used by chemists today.

alkali: Any soluble substance that can neutralize acids to form salts. Also called a base. Sodium bicarbonate, or baking soda, is the most common edible alkali found in kitchens.

amino acids: Molecules made up of carbon, hydrogen, oxygen, nitrogen, and sometimes sulfur that link together into chains to form proteins. When protein is digested, it is broken down into its amino acids and then the amino acids can be reconnected to make up the kind of protein needed by the digester.

atom: The smallest particle of an element that still has the chemical properties of that element. Atoms of one element can combine with atoms of one or more other elements to produce compounds.

bacteria: Microscopic one-celled organisms that have no chlorophyll. Bacteria are found almost everywhere on earth, including in and on the human body. Some bacteria are harmful and cause diseases, but others are beneficial, such as the bacteria that turn milk into cheese.

base: Any compound that can react with an acid to neutralize it and form a salt. Base solutions are bitter and can also conduct electricity. Baking soda when dissolved in water is a base. Also called alkali.

bromelain: An enzyme found in fresh pineapple that breaks down proteins.

buffer: A substance that can absorb acidic or basic molecules and take them out of solution.

calorie: The amount of heat needed to raise one gram of water one degree Celsius. A food calorie is 1,000 calories, or the amount needed to raise 1,000 grams of water one degree Celsius. The diet for the average active adult is figured to be 2,000 calories a day.

caramelization: The breaking down of sugars by heat, which produces simpler compounds that have a brownish color.

carbohydrate: A substance made up of carbon, hydrogen, and oxygen with two hydrogen atoms and one oxygen atom for every atom of carbon. Sugar and starch are both carbohydrates.

carrageenan: A food additive that is extracted from sun-dried Irish moss seaweed. It is used to keep liquid from seeping out of milk-based puddings.

cell: The smallest unit of a living thing. Cells are made up of a substance called protoplasm surrounded by a thin membrane.

cell membrane: The outer skin of a cell.

cellulose: A carbohydrate contained in the cell walls of plants that helps to support their structure.

chemical reaction: Any change that alters the chemical properties of a substance, or that forms a new substance.

chlorophyll: The green pigment in plants that gives them the ability to make food for themselves through photosynthesis.

cholesterol: A white, waxy substance found in animal fat, blood, and nerve tissue. If too much cholesterol is present in the blood vessels that nourish your heart, it can cause heart disease.

clarify: To make clear or free from impurities.

coagulation: The process by which a liquid becomes a soft semisolid. Coagulation is one way a protein is denatured.

coalesce: To grow together; to merge.

collagen: A solid protein that will not dissolve in water. Collagen is found in cartilage, tendons, ligaments, and bones.

colloid: A homogeneous mixture made up of two phases, the solvent and the solute, in which the particles of the solute are larger than single molecules but are small enough to remain suspended in the mixture permanently. The particles of solute in a colloid are larger than the particles in a solution, but not as large as the particles in a suspension.

compound: A pure substance made up of fixed amounts of two or more different elements. A compound differs from a mixture because the substances forming the compound lose their individual characteristics, and the compound takes on its own, often quite different, characteristics.

continuous: Going on or extending without a break. Describes the solvent phase of a solution or suspension, in which all the particles of the solvent are in contact with one another.

control: The part of an experiment that is used to check or compare results.

crystal: A solid bit of pure matter in which the atoms or molecules are arranged in a definite pattern so that the solid has a regular geometric shape with many sides or faces. Examples are salt and sugar.

decant: To pour off gently, leaving the sediment behind. Decanting is one method used to separate two parts of a suspension.

denature: To change the nature of a protein by adding heat, acid, base, etc., so that the original properties are greatly changed or eliminated.

density: A measure of the mass of an object in proportion to its volume. For example, a block of lead will weigh more than an equal-size block of wood. That means lead is denser than wood.

diffusion: An intermingling of the molecules of liquids or gases. The process by which solute particles move through a solvent to form a solution.

discontinuous: Broken up by interruptions or gaps. Describes the solute phase of a solution or suspension in which the particles are not in contact with one another, but are separated by the solvent.

electrodes: Devices that move electrons in and out of solutions, thus allowing a flow of electricity to complete a circuit. Batteries have two electrodes. The cathode has a negative charge and the anode has a positive charge. You can see the ends of an electrode marked + or − on any battery.

electromagnetic radiation: Waves of energy that radiate through space, including light waves, radio waves, X rays, and microwaves.

element: The simplest form of pure matter. There are ninety-eight naturally occurring elements on the earth and twenty-two man-made elements with another six that have been identified but not yet named. All the man-made elements are radioactive and exist for a very short time before decaying into something else.

emulsifying agent: A substance that will keep two immiscible liquids from separating, creating an emulsion (a permanent suspension).

enzyme: A complex protein found in living things that controls chemical reactions without being changed itself.

fermentation: A chemical change in sugars brought about by the enzymes of living organisms, such as yeast. The transformation of grape juice to wine is a good example.

flocculation: The process of drawing impurities out of a substance by collecting them in bunches.

fructose: A simple sugar found in fruit.

gelatin: A jelly-like, soluble protein derived from collagen by heating it with water. When gelatin cools, it forms a clear semisolid.

gelatinization: The process by which a substance swells when it is heated with water.

glucose: A simple sugar found in fruits, green plants, and blood.

gluten: A protein that can be developed from two substances found in wheat and other grains under conditions of warmth, moisture, and massaging (kneading). Gluten gives dough a tough, elastic quality.

homogeneous: Composed of similar or identical parts. In the study of fluids, it describes a solution or colloid in which the solute is evenly distributed throughout the solvent.

hygroscopic: Describes a substance that absorbs moisture from the air.

immiscible: Describes a liquid that cannot be mixed or blended with another liquid. Immiscible liquids, like oil and water, will not form a solution.

indicator: A substance that changes its color or some other property when combined with a solution in which an acid or base is present. For example, litmus paper is an indicator that turns blue when dipped in a base, and pink when dipped in acid.

lactic acid: A waste product of bacteria that feed off lactose.

lactose: A simple sugar found in milk.

magnetron: A device that uses a magnet to make electrons move rapidly in a circular path. Found in microwave ovens.

Maillard reaction: The browning of foods at a dry heat that causes sugars to react with amino acids, producing flavorful molecules with a slightly sweet taste.

matter: Anything that has weight and takes up space. Matter can usually be classified as a solid, a liquid, or a gas and is made up of atoms and molecules. One important property of

matter is density, which equals mass divided by volume.

microbe: A microscopic living thing such as a bacterium. Microbes are often associated with disease or with fermentation. Most microbes are single cells.

microwave: A type of energy that causes the water molecules in a substance to increase their movement, thereby raising the temperature of the substance.

molecule: The smallest particle of a substance that can exist and still retain the characteristics of the substance. The molecule of an element consists of one atom or two or more similar atoms, while the molecule of a compound consists of two or more different atoms.

Nutrition Facts label: A summary of the nutritional value of a food as published on the packaging of that food. It includes the percentage of the daily requirement for each nutrient (based on a 2,000-calorie-per-day diet) and the ingredients present in processed food in order of the greatest quantity to the smallest.

optically active: Describes a substance that has the ability to rotate polarized light.

optics: The science of the nature and properties of light and vision.

osmosis: The movement of molecules of a solvent through a membrane that separates two solutions. The process by which water is absorbed into roots. The direction of flow is from the area of greater concentration of water to the area of lesser concentration of water. Thus water flows into mineral-containing living plant tissue to crisp them up and flows out of cucumber slices that have been soaking in salt water.

oxidation: The chemical reaction of a substance with oxygen.

pasteurization: A method of killing harmful microbes in dairy products, wine, and beer by heating them to denature the protein in the microbes.

photosynthesis: The process by which green plants make sugar from water and carbon dioxide in the air in the presence of chlorophyll, using light energy.

pigment: A natural substance that gives color to the tissues of plants and animals.

plane: A flat surface that has no thickness. It extends forever in two dimensions and has no edges.

polarized light: Light with light rays all vibrating in the plane. Normal light contains rays vibrating in all directions.

polarizer: A lens, say of a pair of sunglasses, that filters light so that when ordinary light passes through, only light that is traveling in a single plane emerges from the lens. Since most glare is horizontally polarized light, a sunglass lens is positioned to block it. If you look at glare coming off a car window in the summer with polarized lenses, most of it is blocked. However, if you turn your head sideways so your glasses are now vertical, the glare will reappear.

precipitate: Insoluble solid particles that form in a liquid as the result of a chemical reaction.

protein: A complex compound made up of amino acids. Proteins are found in all animal or plant matter and are essential to the diet of animals. There can be hundreds of amino acids in a single protein molecule. The bending and folding of amino acid chains gives protein molecules unusual shapes that are a key to the ways they function in living things.

protoplasm: The living material of all cells.

puree: A suspension of food particles in a liquid, for example: pea soup or tomato sauce.

rennin: An enzyme, found in the stomachs of mammals, which will denature milk protein. This enzyme is commercially distributed under the name rennet.

saturated solution: A solution that has absorbed as much of a solute as possible at a given temperature.

serial dilution: A systematic way of varying the amount of water in a solution.

simple sugar: A sugar that contains only five or six carbon atoms.

sol: The liquid stage of a colloid, such as gelatin, dissolved in water. When cooled, it sets into the gel form.

solute: The discontinuous phase of a solution.

solution: A homogeneous mixture with two phases, the solvent and the solute, in which the particles of the solute are the size of single molecules and disperse into the solvent permanently so that the mixture remains homogeneous, or evenly mixed.

solvent: A substance that dissolves another substance. The continuous phase of a solution.

specific gravity: The density of an object compared to the density of water. The density of water is 1 gram per cubic centimeter or 1. All objects with a specific gravity of less than one will float. All with a specific gravity greater than one will sink. Good matzo balls have a specific gravity less than one. You can also compare the specific gravities of packaged breakfast cereals. Note that once they absorb liquid, they sink.

starch: A complex carbohydrate found in potatoes, rice, corn, wheat, and other foods. A starch molecule is made of long chains of simple sugar molecules.

substrate: The material a microbe uses for food.

sucrose: Table sugar. Sucrose is a two-molecule chain with one molecule of glucose and one molecule of fructose.

sugar: A sweet, crystalline, water-soluble compound made of carbon, hydrogen, and oxygen. It provides energy for living things.

supersaturated solution: A clear solution that contains more solute than would normally dissolve at a certain temperature.

suspension: A mixture with two phases, the solvent and the solute, in which the particles of the solute are much larger than a single molecule. These particles can be distributed throughout the solvent when stirred but do not dissolve. The particles will eventually separate from the solvent and either sink or float, depending on their specific gravities.

titration: A method used to measure solutions based on the concentration of particular substances. It can be used to measure the strength of an acid, an alkali, or a sugar solution.

Tyndall effect: A phenomenon in which particles of a certain size reflect light. You can see the Tyndall effect in a beam of sunlight in a dusty room. Dust particles are big enough to reflect the light, while air molecules are too small. As a result you can see the beam when looking at it sideways. Another example is headlights in fog.

water vacuole: Surrounded by a membrane and contains water, along with some enzymes. One of its most important jobs is to maintain the "crispness" of a plant cell. When it loses water, the cell and the plant droop.

xylem: A stiff, long strand, found in plants such as celery that carries water from the roots of the plant to the leaves.

EQUIVALENT MEASURES

pinch = less than ¼ teaspoon

dash = 2 or 3 drops

1 tablespoon = 3 teaspoons = ½ ounce

1 ounce = 2 tablespoons

1 cup = 16 tablespoons = 8 ounces = ½ pint (liquid)

1 quart = 2 pints = 4 cups = 32 ounces

1 gallon = 4 quarts = 8 pints = 16 cups = 128 ounces

1 pound = 16 ounces

1 cup broth = 1 bouillon cube dissolved in 1 cup water

1 quarter-pound stick of butter = ½ cup = 8 tablespoons

1 envelope of gelatin = 1 tablespoon

SELECTED BIBLIOGRAPHY

Hillman, Howard. *Kitchen Science: A Guide to Knowing the Hows and Whys for Fun and Success in the Kitchen*. Revised edition. Boston: Houghton Mifflin Company, 1989.

McGee, Harold. *On Food and Cooking: The Science and Lore of the Kitchen*. New York: Macmillan, 1984.

———. *The Curious Cook*. San Francisco: North Point Press, 1990.

Moss, Michael. *Salt Sugar Fat: How the Food Giants Hooked Us*. New York: Random House, 2014.

This, Hervé. *Molecular Gastronomy: Exploring the Science of Flavor*. Translated by Malcolm DeBevoise. New York: Columbia University Press, 2006.

———. *Kitchen Mysteries: Revealing the Science of Cooking*. Translated by Jody Gladding. New York: Columbia University Press, 2010.

Touissant-Samat, Maguelonne. *A History of Food*. Translated by Anthea Bell. Cambridge, MA: Blackwell Publishing, 1992.

Trager, James. *The Food Book*. New York: Avon, 1972.

INDEX